Road

Diverged

THE PATHS OF FAITH FEW WILL TAKE

By GARRY HARPER, M.Th.S

Preface

This book's title is something borrowed from the famous poet, Robert Frost, and his poem, *The Road Not Taken*. It was one of the first classical poems I ever memorized. I remember the spirit of adventure rising up within me as I considered Frost's clear intent.

Choosing to take a path that has become overgrown from disuse is a risky thing. Taking it, however, will make all the difference. To step forward into its uncertainty begs the nagging question of whether or not this particular path isn't in use for good reason. Perhaps wild animals await there. It may come to an abrupt end.

The path leading to economic and political policies that fairly reflect Christian theology is like that. It has not been used for quite some time. There are dangers to avoid not the least of which is the temptation to marginalize those who do not share the Christian faith.

One thing is clear, however. Social and cultural paths (all of them) ultimately come to an end. They all end in time. For the Christian, time is limited because our theology takes into account God's plan to someday bring time to an end for a final judgment. After that, there will be an existence that is no longer bound by time – it will be timelessness rather than a prolongation of time into infinity.

What is the difference? In one case (prolongation) time still exists and therefore humanity will continue to be bound by it and, presumably, the other dimensional limitations we now experience in what we call space. The other (timelessness) indicates a new sort of creation where humanity will no longer be bound by the "cause and effect" world of space and time. It will be a place where faith expands beyond the boundaries of the cosmos, taking us into the domain of God himself. We will *meet* Jesus there.

Realizing that all paths in our cosmos have an end the Christian has to consider whether or not to travel the relatively insignificant paths of economics or politics. This book deeply explores that question and comes to the conclusion that Christians must do what God placed us here (within space and time) to do.

This book will open the possibility that the economic and political path of the Christian isn't where the media and many vocal Christians think it is. It isn't the road most travelled.

Well-Worn Paths

It is no secret that Christians choose to be different; but why are they so different from each other? The existence of denominations demonstrate that divisions, some harmful and others less so, continue to separate Christians on Sunday and confuse non-Christians every day of the week. One would imagine that the God Christians describe would have, by this time (over 2,000 years since Jesus) intervened with some kind of sign to halt his follower's drive toward division.

Perhaps he is content to let the evolution of belief continue toward some end that Christians simply cannot see. The divisions are real and some are really destructive when it comes to generating a common goal for the economic, political and cultural behavior of all Christians. If there is hope for bridging the gaps it will have to come from those inside its ranks. If that is to happen it will require consistent and determined leadership from a wide spectrum of leaders.

The sources of division can be historically traced first to doctrinal disputes and secondarily to those differences that arose through centuries of political and cultural upheaval around the globe.

It's best to begin with an understanding of what doctrine is and its relationship to theology. They are not the same thing although they are often used interchangeably in conversations creating a bit of confusion. Theology is strictly rooted in a declaration of faith. It is foundational in that it expresses that which is accepted as fact without reliance on the "cause and effect" evidence that is an essential element in science and logic. Theology supersedes logic in the sense that it is substituted for fact at the point where logic cannot find the first "cause."

In the case of humanity, the search for meaning – the answer to why we are here – brings every human to a point of placing faith in one's self as the ultimate arbiter of right and wrong or in what Anselm described as, "that which nothing greater can be conceived" – or "God." Without evidence to suggest otherwise the great theoretical physicist, Steven Hawking, explained that all that exists in the universe "began" from a point where all that we are able see appears to have come into being out of "nothing."

It is at this point that all of humanity must take a "leap of faith" in describing who or what could bring something out of nothing. For Christians, theology is answering that question with an acknowledgement that humanity is a created thing with personhood (self determination) but that there exists a Creator that is beyond our ability to properly conceive.

Doctrine, on the other hand, *is* a function of logic. It follows quickly on the heels of theology and attempts to explain truths derived from the premise that God does exist. Taken together with the evidence he has provided all of us through his Sovereign intervention into the lives of humanity, Christians rationally develop doctrine.

For Christians the process of formulating doctrine has been and continues to be reactive. The historical development of Christian doctrine can be discovered in numerous volumes written by highly capable historians and theologians. But it is dynamic. In other words, Christians continue to explore truth to this day and doctrines are the principle reason divisions exist between Christian communities. Some doctrines are weightier than others and have their origin in the biblical writings of the Apostles. These truths are so widely accepted by Christendom, that they are called "orthodox" beliefs.

Since the early second century Christianity's "founding fathers" actively defended orthodoxy through a process of carefully examining developing beliefs against the authorities of the faith. The authorities of the faith are generally accepted to be one of three: the apostolic teaching (first delivered to successive generations of Christians orally), the Canon of Scripture (authoritatively establish during the fourth century) and the traditions of the Universal Church (Catholicism) where precedents were established through councils of bishops and other Church leaders.

Once the Roman Catholic Church was safely established and relatively free of persecution (around A.D. 325) doctrines were routinely measured against the Catholic Church's accepted authorities. Beliefs that were inconsistent with authority were considered heresy and sometimes severely persecuted.

However, not all beliefs that were considered heresy disappeared. Some were so successfully argued as to foster the development of new branches within Christianity. These often enjoyed their own definition of orthodoxy and dominated regional areas within the geographic domain of the Roman Catholic Church. In fact, some ideas that were at first considered heretical were subsequently accepted as truth. One famous example would be the belief, first postulated by Copernicus, that the earth was round rather than flat.

The views that radically reshaped Christianity into what is seen today happened during the Reformation that separated Christianity into the camps of Protestant and Catholic doctrine. Not coincidentally the Scriptures of Christianity were made available to the common man shortly before Luther's challenge reached the Pope's ears. The availability of Scripture led to a boom in doctrinal argument and discovery. That discovery and the ideas embodied therein are the main reason there are divisions among Christians to this day.

So, for roughly 2,000 years Christians have argued with one another over large and small areas of doctrine. It is not likely that anyone will emerge during the next century to settle all of these differences once and for all – least of which this writer. However, those who are willing to carefully consider the basis of division can unite around the *theology* of Christianity. With that as a foundation, Christians can determine those ideas that best serve humanity in terms of economic and political policy.

Christians already have a majority position among the various theologies represented in America. It is true that there are Christians who seem to be more vocal than others and may represent a narrower doctrinal view than many who are self-described but perhaps less ardent Christians. But it is possible that the common ground of theology can unite American Christians around an economic and political agenda that will form a new and powerful majority in America.

Please be quick to understand that forming this kind of political power does not have intolerance of other faiths embedded within its theology. Quite the contrary – one of Christianity's basic theological tenets is the human entitlement of "natural rights" granted by the Creator. These rights were enumerated in America's Declaration of Independence. God's gift of "free will" to humanity is fundamental to Christian theology – as will be explained – and any Christian majority that emerges as a political force in America could only violate that freedom at the expense of their own deeply held faith.

In fact, it is Christians in America who are pressured to secularize their fundamental beliefs and have experienced, first hand, the assault of American humanism – the fundamental belief in humanity's preeminence in the universe. This is considered an assault because humanism's principle theology places faith in humanity rather than the God of

Christianity and rejects moral absolutes that are the foundation of an orderly society.

American Christians (including those who are only nominally "Christian") find themselves ranging completely across the nation's current political spectrum from left to right. In spite of this there exists an opportunity – let's call it a "narrow" path – for American Christians to carefully reconsider the doctrinal differences that divide us and formulate reasonable political and cultural actions that fairly express the will of God and the teachings of Jesus or – our common theology.

In order to tackle this monumental task it is best to start with the most divisive doctrines first. After all, if we cannot emerge from that discussion with unity of political purpose there will be no point in reading or writing anything further. To do this as practically as possible, two major elements of Christianity's divisions will be discussed: First, the issue of God's will over and against the supposed free will of man and secondly the role of Church government (or polity) in terms of how individual denominations and churches choose to govern themselves internally.

It has to be stressed that these two doctrinal positions are by no means the only things that divide Christians. They are, however, the most visible elements in describing why some Christians choose one particular denomination or church over another. It also must be stated that a complete explanation of the various viewpoints should be obtained from theological and doctrinal works expressly written to shed light on these subjects. The attempt here to explain the various viewpoints simply cannot be exhaustive and this work is aimed to impact a broad spectrum of Christians who may or may not even be fully aware of the differences they might have with the group of Christians meeting across town from them.

The most reasonable beginning point is the doctrine that explains the person of God. Theologically, it is a given that God cannot be contained or fully examined within the realm of logic itself or the mind of man. Logic is, after all, limited to the fields of creation (time and space) where we find numerous examples of cause and effect. Within the realms of our experience humanity draws conclusions based on elemental observations. For example if, a = b, and b = c, then logic helps us conclude that "a" is also equal to "c." Logic starts with a concept that is already defined or an effect for which a cause needs to be discovered. What if something defies definition or even explanation? What if there appears to be no cause to a particular effect?

That is exactly what happens when humanity attempts to consider God and define him. In order to have effected creation it is logical (or at least practical) that God himself existed in some way beyond, outside of, or apart from the thing he created. Theologians use the word, "infinitude," to describe the transcendence of God over creation or "Sovereignty" to describe his authority to affect anything within or without the created universe. Sovereignty is more commonly used to describe an earthly king or queen and expresses, at least in part, the right of the monarch to make completely arbitrary decisions that suit their will. God's will (the thing Christians pray for when reciting the "Lord's prayer") is necessarily beyond our comprehension even though his actions have been communicated – sometimes explained – to us through his prophets, Scripture, and through the advent of his Son into our world – Jesus the Messiah or Christ.

In attempting to understand the will of God humans ultimately have to account for the presence of "evil" in the world. Scripture explains that creation, as it existed prior to Adam and Eve's sin, was thoroughly "good." Still, within the Garden of Eden, there was a creature (apparently embodied within the serpent) that was bent on displacing God as Sovereign. Where did he come from? Clearly God created this being. Does this make God responsible for "evil" in creation? The point of this question can be reduced to a very simplistic level. If God's will is completely contained within his person – if he is truly Sovereign – then within our created minds it is only logical to conclude that humanity itself has nothing to say or do about its collective future nor can we comprehend the motive behind God's creation of that serpent (the devil).

As creatures, we are all going around a sort of created merry-go-round with a defined beginning and a defined end. If God is ultimately responsible for evil in the creation then humanity cannot be held accountable for its individual or collective behavior. And yet, since God *is* Sovereign and the creator of all we can experience, we *can* be destined to any particular end he desires whether that is salvation from the evil or damnation.

Compounding the problem (as if what was just covered isn't enough) the Bible describes God's decision to allow humanity the freedom to choose whether or not to actually acknowledge and obey him. The question is whether or not that freedom is *real*. Logic would dictate that the will of God is irresistible and that any freedom humanity has to "choose" is practically ineffective. The choice, from a logical perspective, is absurd.

While it appears that humanity does, in fact, have the ability to choose whether or not to acknowledge God and obey his laws, it also appears that God would not actually be beyond our ability to conceive if he weren't ultimately responsible for whatever it is that we do. From the perspective of humanity it is only logical to assume one of two possibilities.

Either we actually do have a free will and God has somehow elected to limit his own will to respond to ours (something that makes him somewhat less than totally "Sovereign") or our freedom to choose God is simply an illusion he created to either humor himself or those humans who enjoy wagging their fingers at one another while judging themselves somehow more righteous than those to whom their fingers point.

In terms of Christian doctrine this conundrum deeply affected the means of salvation. Christians wanted to know (logically) just how they were saved from their sin and disobedience. The question itself was complicated by the culture in which

Christianity existed throughout its history. How so?

In the early years of the Church, during the time before the written Scriptures were available, salvation was taught to be an act of God's grace wherein he responded to expressions of faith by the individual human. In other words, it was believed that humans had a part in the process by exercising their freedom to choose God's way. Through sheer faith humanity could simply choose to acknowledge God, acknowledge sinfulness, repent and be saved by his grace.

It was evident from the Apostles' teaching that humanity had a part in the process as humans were encouraged to believe and repent. On the other hand, it was also clear that the decision to forgive and save was God's and his alone. As Scripture and the doctrine it contained was established over the ensuing two centuries, salvation continued to baffle those within and without Christianity when viewed through the lens of logic. Some opted to consider the process exclusively a preemptive decision of God and labeled that doctrine "monergism." In their view, God predestined some for salvation and some for damnation but this was his right as Sovereign and Creator of the universe. God, in this case, acted alone in the event; he acted monergistically.

On the other hand, those who believed that some level of human participation was essential in the process of salvation called their doctrine "synergism," suggesting that salvation was a kind of cooperation with God and that salvation was therefore dependent on the will of man. Ironically it was the writings of the Apostle Paul to which *both* groups made reference when defending their position. As Christianity expanded those who favored synergism over monergism held the majority position among believers.

By the fourth century Christianity became the recognized and official state religion of the Roman Empire. As its power grew the Church eventually vested complete authority in the bishop of Rome (the Pope) and the Catholic Church under his leadership asserted itself as the dispensary of salvation and the vehicle through which either eternal life was granted or condemnation pronounced.

Even though the teaching of Christianity clearly showed that salvation was a free gift of grace and God's response to human faith the Church's role in extending forgiveness through the confessional process soon came to make the process more about politics than theology. Salvation was made available to only those who were in good standing with the Church and the Church (which was rapidly becoming a political organization) began to dispense eternal security in response to *behaviors* that had little to do with faith in God and much more to do with the treasure one was willing to impart back to the Church.

By the time of the Reformation the Catholic Church was steeped in a process where salvation was "earned" through charitable giving and through works of righteousness. As the Scriptures themselves became more readily available and translated into common languages the complexity of the arguments on both sides once again surfaced among theologians and those who broke away from the Catholic tradition restarted the struggle over predestination and free will.

The protestant movement was essentially a rebellion against the Roman Catholic Church's distribution of salvation and eternal reward for "good behavior." Its proponents sought instead to make salvation the sole domain of God. Luther, Zwingli and Calvin opted to support monergism defining salvation as something that only God could do through his grace. Even though God responded to man's faith the protestant movement generally believed that even faith itself was a gift from God making God alone the arbiter of our fate.

All of these differing views, however, were in one way or another steeped in humanity's attempt to discover God's will and purposes through **logic**. The power of the human mind to conceive of propositions that can be tested in the laboratory of life continues to drive us toward a description of God with which all Christians can have comfort. <u>But what if logic is not capable of accurately describing God or our role in salvation?</u>

In America today there are nearly as many denominations of Christianity as letters in the alphabet. Each has a following of varying strength and nearly all have been founded upon a principle departure from another group of Christians where <u>logical</u> conclusions brought about division. There are Calvinistic denominations who thoroughly believe in his logical description of double predestination – where God has both elected to save some and elected to condemn others. Calvinism teaches there is nothing one can do to earn salvation and likewise nothing one can do to lose it. Humility marks those who hold this view; they are not willing to take credit for anything God has done for them nor do they want the safety of their salvation to be dependent on their ability to remain behaviorally sinless.

Then there were also Arminian Protestants, followers of Jacob Arminius, who believed strongly that humanity does have a role in salvation through the exercise of free will. Today these denominations actively evangelize through missionary efforts that seek to bring the message of God's grace to all those who will simply "cooperate" with God's will by truly believing.

Some of these denominations are a bit more legalistic in their view of human behavior because, for them, it is just as easy to lose one's salvation through chronic disobedience as it was to get the free gift in the first place. These two groups, along with a few denominations somewhere in the middle, define American Christianity as it relates to the subject of God's will versus mankind's freedom of choice, and whether or not God acts alone in our salvation (monergism) or cooperates with our free will (synergism). All of the denominations strive for a doctrine that is *logically* consistent.

American Christians, regardless of their doctrinal position on synergism versus monergism, do find some areas of common agreement in the world of politics and culture.

Many are willing to accept that differences in doctrine do not have to be essential disagreements in theology.

On the other hand these groups, like the rest of America, tend to place themselves all along the spectrum of political thought as it is expressed in terms of left and right – the liberal and conservative viewpoint. Is there a logical basis for Christianity's diversity of political thought? The answer might be found in the breakdown of denominations that follow "liberal" and "conservative" religious practices and doctrine.

Here the words liberal and conservative apply to religious rather than political action. "Liberal Christians" tend to accept authoritative statements beyond the Bible. These statements come from church leaders, historians, theologians and the social and political culture in which liberal Christians practice their faith. "Conservative Christians" tend to accept the Bible alone as the definitive authority for doctrine and practice. They tend to force political and cultural considerations through the lens of a literal interpretation of the Bible.

If one were to think of the way conservatives in politics adhere exclusively to an originalist view of the Constitution and the way liberals in politics consider current cultural realities and/or precedents outside of the Constitution, they would have a fairly clear example of how Christians are labeled either "conservative" or "liberal" in their theology.

Conservative Christians have, historically, been more proactive in politics. Their religious zeal for a literal interpretation of the Bible easily translates over to dogmatism about the literal interpretation of the Constitution. This group is seen more often in the media perhaps explaining why there is a perception within and without Christianity that most American Christians are political conservatives as well.

There are exceptions to the generalizations that follow and it must be said that political ideas within a single local church will still vary. Having said that, here are some broad generalizations about Christians in terms of their view of God's will versus man's free choice and its impact on social, cultural and political thought:

Calvinist or Monergistic Christians

> Calvinist Christians favor monergism, the view that God acts alone in saving or condemning individuals. They tend to be mostly conservative in politics as well.

With a highly defined view of God's ultimate sovereignty over the universe these Christians have a tendency to see God's ways in purely black and white terms with few shades of gray. God's will over the universe is irretrievably set and those who come to acknowledge him do so because God's will is functionally irresistible.

Politically, these Christians are active in seeking a return to traditional Biblical values as they relate to the preeminence of family and a faith in God's purposes for America. These Christians tend to see America as a beacon of light to the rest of the world. They decry the demolition of family values among the left or liberal wings of American politics and are most comfortable when they are surrounded by like-minded Christians.

Those who disagree with their interpretation of history and/or their view of God are generally considered to be among the billions of humans (throughout history up to the current time) who, because God did not choose them for salvation, are lost. The majority of these Christians will say that Scripture alone is their final arbiter of theological debate and will go to great lengths to assure that the translation of Scripture is accurate in reflecting the original intent of the Hebrew and Greek writers who wrote under the inspiration of God.

They will invoke the will of God when outlining what Scripture has to say about humanity's future. There, in Scripture, they will point to the great calamity that is destined to fall upon the earth and especially those who have rejected Christ. They are not, however, completely devoid of compassion and are, in fact, responsible for many of the world's largest historical missionary efforts outside of the Catholic Church. These Christians seem, to the world at large, to be largely intolerant of humanity's historic shift toward individualism and humanism. They will defend themselves, however, by stating that it is not their right to be "tolerant."

They believe the Word of God is just that...his Word – with a capital "W." They are not called to question its content nor defend it. If, for example, God's Word wholly condemns homosexuality, then it is not up to them to be tolerant of homosexuals or the gay and lesbian political agenda. They see all of humanity as a subsidiary force of God – as part of his overall creation – in subjection to his overarching will and eternal plan.

They are routinely accused of bigotry in various forms although racial bigotry is certainly not a part of their dogma. That is not to say that racial bigotry never existed within their ranks but it is no longer defended as it might have been during and shortly after the Civil War. This group now includes many minorities but is nevertheless completely intolerant of divergent views of God or his purposes if the views in question cannot be supported by the totality of Scripture. Because of their strict adherence to Scripture as the sole arbiter of right and wrong, Calvinistic Christians are frequently parodied in the public media.

They are too frequently categorized as intellectually deficient even though there is enormous evidence this group represents some of the most highly educated Christians in the world. Having provided the intellectual support for the break from the Roman Catholic Church this group tends to spend more time and money on Christian education and home schooling. They have been historically less tolerant of Catholicism but accept Catholics as great partners in support of pro-life positions.

Calvinistic churches trend toward an "episcopal" or "presbyterian" form of church government. That is they tend to have pastors that are appointed as opposed to being popularly elected by the local congregation.

Arminian or Synergistic Christians

Arminian Christians tend to have a more synergistic view of salvation and a greater confidence in the free will of humanity; they often take a higher view of humanity's capacity for good as well. Whereas one tenet of Calvinism is the "depravity" of man, these believers have a difficult time condemning so many humans to hell – particularly those who may not have had the opportunity to hear the Gospel. It's one reason they are very missionary minded.

Christians who hold a synergistic view of salvation are sometimes called, "free-will" Christians. Their view of the nature of man is somewhat different than Calvinists. They agree that all humanity is flawed by sin but are more likely to think "sin" is the result of each individual person making rebellious decisions in their own lives rather than being "born a sinner." As such, they also tend to have no trouble taking *credit* for their more "heavenly" actions. In this group of Christians, there is a certain pride taken in their decision to follow Christ and a sometimes inordinate pride in their versions of personal holiness – actions that tend to display their everyday choices to follow God's laws.

Since their behavior is so important to their ultimate salvation, these Christians may trend toward political liberalism. Progressive politics are viewed as being more personally compassionate and sharing from their abundance reflects positively on their sense of personal value.

Arminian Christians also include those who place great significance on "experiential" Christianity – where one's life experiences take on a level of authority sometimes equal to what they read in Scripture. Christians who see a significant role for their own will in the course of knowing God often seek an ongoing (every day) revelation of God's personal will for their individual personal life.

They see God active in everything they personally do and love to cooperate with his will. As such, it is not at all unlikely that some of these Christians will gravitate to liberal politics and favor the expansion of federal programs that reach out to individuals who are hurting with aid or assistance.

These types of Christians also tend to see the teachings of Jesus exclusively related to life as it is experienced here on planet Earth. Although they will acknowledge that Jesus vigorously taught about the "Kingdom of Heaven" they often see an equal emphasis on bringing that "kingdom" to earth here and now.

Among this group of Christians are some groups of "Charismatics" who experience a wholly unique form of cooperation with God as they exercise various "gifts of the Spirit" such as prophecy, healing, and speaking in tongues. Charismatics are just as likely to be liberal as conservative in terms of American politics. This is the case because they tend to adhere to a legalistic view of morality and are constrained by their terms of salvation to remain "saved" through constant obedience.

On the other hand, they are much more in tune with a kind of compassionate empathy for fellow travelers who find themselves ensnared with sinful habits. Synergistic Christians span the full range of choices in Church government but have a much greater tendency to form democracies where the local church is independent from a governing body. These kinds of churches are called "congregational" because they tend to self-govern through popularly elected leaders.

While these two potential descriptions of Christians are based on logical conclusions when considering the impact of God's will over or with humanity's free choice, these descriptions remain generalizations. Most Christians that read the foregoing will probably find portions of each description with which they personally identify. But all of this is based on the same *logic* that Christianity has used for 2,000 years to explain the doctrines of the Bible.

What if logic is simply inadequate? Is there another possibility here that American Christians should at least entertain as a possible ground for more political and cultural unity? Is it plausible, for example that God remains above human logic but has willed human logic to govern certain aspects of life within the space and time continuum he created?

Could God have a comprehensive plan for the entire universe, its history, and the course of his human creation that nevertheless concedes the operation of free will within that creation? Can the will of man be completely significant to individual men while remaining a subsidiary of God's ultimate aims?

It seems altogether incongruous for us to conceive that our free will is even meaningful if *all the while* God has already cast the die against some. And yet, even the foregoing statement shows a presupposition in the words, "all the while."

We are bound by time.

It is part of our very existence and is shaped by the laws of physics set into place when God spoke everything into existence.

God, however, is not bound by time. It is nothing more or less than a part of the same creation in which we find humanity. Humanity is bound by time and our logic is therefore subservient to the experiences we think are "real" within its boundaries. Within time, and we all live within time, our choices are immanently important – to us and, apparently, to God as well. Remarkably, we can affect our relationship with God and our place and standing with him in that existence that is outside the limitations of both space and time.

It is not at all remarkable that God "knows" what will happen within the very time bubble he created. It would seem a given that he knows all of its eventualities as one who exists outside of it limitations. God is not limited to matter or anti-matter as each is simply a part of his creation. Black holes do not perplex God but the very thought of them is both perplexing and entertaining to humanity. Our space time limitations are what bind us to a world of logical conclusions based exclusively on what we are able to perceive and experience in nature's cause and effect relationship.

It is entirely possible, even plausible, that neither monergism (Calvinism) nor synergism (Arminianism) accurately describes man's free will when set against the will of God. Within the limitations of space and time it is absurd to claim that humanity has no choice when it comes to behavior or beliefs. At this very moment I am fully capable of typing anything for the next word in this sentence. Yet it is equally absurd to think that God (a being beyond which nothing greater can be conceived) wouldn't know what it is that I will type next. Does this knowledge preclude me from typing an "e" or an "a?" It is clear that our logic is far too limiting on God. It is also clear that his sovereignty is too magnificent for us to logically comprehend or imagine.

On the other hand, what is clear is that God has a character of grace that is also beyond our imagination. Not only did he create all that we can experience within time and space but it would seem that he created us with a unique capacity to understand it logically.

It is as though nothing is beyond our reach of understanding within creation even while it is entirely possible that nothing outside of creation is humanly discernible. The majesty of God's grace is evident in the possibility that we can somehow know him in a limited way within this creation and accept a free gift of knowing him more completely in whatever it is that exist beyond what we can logically know from this – our limited perspective.

In a real sense, all of this is God's doing. Those who hold to monergism (Calvinism) are right about that. Humanity cannot take credit for anything and most especially we cannot take credit for advancing our own salvation. Still, the synergist is also right. We do have a choice and it appears that our choice is actually meaningful. If, like the Calvinist think, our choice is still an irresistible choice brought on by God's sovereign election to give us the faith, then that capacity of God's character is operating wholly outside of the time and space in which we exist. If, like the Arminian, we think our choice actually changes God's mind, then that can be true within the space and time of our existence but doesn't impact God's unchangeable nature outside of the space and time he created for our benefit.

Christians, then, should unite around the magnificence of our God. We are somehow very important to his will in the space and time in which we, his creation, exist. Our choices DO matter. Likewise we have a promise that goes beyond what we can logically comprehend in the existence that is to come for those who place their faith in him and his purposes.

What would that unity look like? If all Christians, Protestants and Catholics alike, united around the idea that our choices within this creation matter and that God's will here on earth should be done, what would that look like? Before answering that we have to return to the second area that divides Christians – the political and cultural developments that have influenced Christians throughout history.

The Cultural and Political History of Christianity

What is it that constitutes a "cultural" divide? Here's one example: Jesus was a Jew. He came into our world as something different. He was, according to Christian theology, both fully human and fully God. In his humanity he came, as promised, through the lineage of David, Abraham, Noah and Adam. As a "son" of David, Jesus was a Jew from the tribe of Judah. He was born into a culture that expressed itself in ways that would seem extremely foreign to modern day Christians. His was a patriarchal society – built around men and specifically the father of the household.

Early Christians were primarily Jews as well and continued to live for some time within the structures of Jewish society in Jerusalem and the reaches of Judaism beyond that city's boundaries. Christians were naturally inclined to follow a patriarchal form of family organization and the kind of society that form engendered.

Men were decision makers, they were authoritarian in the sense that the ultimate buck of responsibility stopped at their feet. Are we, as modern day Christians, supposed to return to a patriarchal form of culture? What about the fact that the culture of Jesus' Jerusalem included the ownership of slaves? What facets of cultural organization are we to hold as definitive of Christianity?

Within a few decades of the Church's founding in Jerusalem it had grown and spread throughout the immediate regions around Palestine. Gentiles, anyone who was not Jewish, began accepting the faith and converting to its theology and the doctrinal practices of its Judaistic roots.

At first, these doctrines included certain elements of Judaism like circumcision for males. Within a few centuries the faith had spread throughout the known world and its expression was certainly impacted by the diversity of cultures it encountered. Its survival was a testament to its flexibility to incorporate divine truth that addressed the condition of humanity within the context of human existence and within the context of different cultures.

Were there things that converts had to accept – things from which they had to separate themselves? They certainly did. Idolatry was forbidden as this was inconsistent with God's historic revelation in the Ten Commandments described in the Old (Jewish) Testament.

Christianity easily crossed cultural borders in its expansion. This is not to say that Christianity merely assumed the faiths it replaced and incorporated them into its own dogma either – even though it is historically accurate to say that some forms of Christianity did incorporate pagan ideas or rituals. Christian orthodoxy and its purity of practice survived through many cultural pressures that could have changed its nature and fundamental faith.

Merging two religions together is call syncretism. It's like synchronizing two watches to read the same time without eliminating one of the watches. While that might have happened in isolation from time to time that was not the aim Jesus envisioned when he called his disciples and sent them out to preach his Gospel.

Different cultures certainly impacted Christianity but the aim was for Christian theology to positively impact all cultures by elevating itself above mere "religious" practice. The orthodoxy of Christianity was evident in spreading the good news that God had intervened in human history to reveal his character and plans for that which would lay beyond the creation of space and time as humans understood it.

History has emphatically shown that political pressures also influenced Christianity's growth and development but God's message given through Jesus – the good news – eclipses generational politics because politics is, after all, limited by space and time – is it not?

The question a Christian has to answer is simply this: Should culture and politics influence Christianity or should Christianity be a mitigating influence within politics and culture? If we hold the truth – the good news – isn't it logical to conclude that within space and time our truth should form a mitigating influence for good over the culture and politics of a world (an entire creation) that is enslaved to sin and corruption?

The word "mitigating" is important here. Since Christians understand that our universe is limited by God's design in terms of space and time, we look forward to our citizenship in God's new kingdom – that which will be experienced at the end of time as we know it. As such, our job in this limited time and space is to mitigate the dangers of sin and its impact on the rest of humanity.

Christians have to ultimately decide where their primary citizenship lies. Scripture is clear that this world, this creation as we know it, will not survive the judgment of God. Are we to take over the cultures and politics of this world by force and impose the will of God on humanity?

It is far more likely that God has other plans for us. Scripture and the teachings of Jesus indicate that our future will include a cataclysmic end to the creation as we know it – and that includes space and time – in fact the entire universe as we currently understand it. While we were instructed to preach the good news of God's ultimate redemption of humanity and the promise of a new existence, we were never instructed to bring that "heaven" onto this earth through cultural or political or even military operations.

Still, we hold the truth and that truth is a powerful force that should be gathered and aimed at getting the message of Christianity out. That could very well mean that part of our responsibility is to form a politically and culturally mitigating force that allows us to get the truth out there more "truthfully."

Without getting into a detailed discourse in history it is safe to simply say that over the past 2,000 years humanity has experienced Christianity's influence through a number of cultures and political environments. During that time the world has seen the transformation of human government from despotic leadership and monarchies to various forms of democratic evolution. As it stands today Christians in America have had the mixed blessing of operating in a mostly democratic environment both in American culture and in the governance of the various Christian denominations.

Roman Catholicism is unique in that its leadership isn't really democratic at all. It remains locked into a form a monarchical leadership with a history dating back to the fourth century. In fact, Catholicism is the only denomination of Christianity that is also considered a nation among the nations of the world.

The Vatican enjoys sovereign immunity among the nations. As the unfortunate disclosure of pedophilia among the Catholic priesthood emerged over the past decade the world has learned that Pope Benedict was in the unique position of administrating discipline in several cases where priests were caught in the crime. His response at the time, a time prior to his becoming Pope, was alleged to have been less than adequate. In an article published on April 23, 2010 in *Newsweek*, Christopher Hitchens wrote that attorneys for Pope Benedict had already signaled that they would invoke "sovereign immunity" if subpoenaed by a Kentucky court.

The world wide status of the Catholic Church as a sovereign nation has elevated it beyond the reach of any national government. This is in stark contrast to any Protestant denomination. Can you imagine the General Superintendent of the Baptist convention invoking a similar defense against a subpoena?

Even in the face of its monarchical structure, American Catholics are so attuned to democracy as to widely disassociate themselves with the Vatican's authority even while continuing to fellowship and take communion in their local parishes. America's political leaders that happen to be Catholic are perhaps the most notorious dodgers of Papal authority.

Among the Protestant denominations, the Episcopal (aka Anglican Church), Presbyterian, Lutheran and Methodists continue to operate with a strong demarcation between its clergy and laity. The clergy benefits from a position of authority over the laity (the people) which is a residual practice from Catholicism. Its clergy are generally assigned to local congregations although there are exceptions to this practice that are, for the most part, changes intended to address the uniquely "American" love affair with democracy in general. Those denominations that are considered more "fundamental" in terms of evangelism have a much greater tendency than either Catholics or the clergy-driven denominations to be wholly democratic in their local church government. Most are "congregational" governments where the local church membership holds popular votes to elect their clergy into service. In many congregational churches the Pastor is only one of several lay-elders with equal authority.

American Christians are accustomed to the power of voting and, even though some may associate with clergy-driven denominations, they continue to "vote" their desires through their voluntary donations that keep the church lights on and its doors open. The cultural and political development within this country predisposes Christians of all denominations to search for ways to personally impact their church just as they influence national politics.

As Christians become more aware of just how God's will works with their own they can build a political and cultural agenda which most of America can support. Does this mean that Christians will (or should) march in lock step to one political agenda? Perhaps not. However it is possible that American Christians can find enough in common with each other to set a broad agenda for the future of an American democracy that acknowledges God's Sovereignty and mankind's free will.

Simply talking about this is admittedly easier than seeing it come to fruition in real life. That is why this book cannot be strictly theoretical. It must be applicable in real life here in America. Finally, it's time to get specific.

Tackling Specific Issues

We live in a society where the news of the day comes to us in short bursts with vivid imagery. Issues are brought to our attention mostly with symbolic depictions that tend to polarize our thinking. Symbols, in essence, evoke emotional responses while lengthy descriptions – especially those that include other viewpoints – tend to make us change the channel. On the one hand American Christians need an emotional boost to get involved. But an emotional boost generally will not have the long term impact of a deeply held belief in something that is true and rationally defended.

Political and religious writers are equally prone to ignore the details and avoid specifics when writing opinion pieces. The aim is to energize but, for American Christians, the energy must be supported by ideas that are specific enough to make a long-term difference. Long term results can only be achieved when the actions are inherently right not just symbolically soothing. All of this means that the idea of an American Christian majority sounds good on paper but can it really "play in Peoria?" As Joan Rivers might say, "Can we talk?"

National Health Care/Insurance

The idea that the federal government should provide health care or at least health insurance for all Americans was first voiced by President Theodore Roosevelt. It was his cousin, however, President Franklin D. Roosevelt, that sought to make it part of his social security system in 1944. Most Americans know that it finally became law here in American in March of 2010 when Congress used a rare form of legislative rule to circumvent a new vote by the Senate on the House amended bill.

Normally the Senate would have had to revote on the changes made by the House. The procedure, a budget reconciliation process, allowed by House rules covering reconciliation of budget amounts in the Senate version, allowed the House to vote on the Senate's bill, with modifications as long as they reduced the deficit. President Obama signed it into law.

As of this writing a majority of Americans (59% according to Rasmussen polling – August 2, 2010) would prefer to have that law repealed even though it has not even gone into effect. The Congressional sleight of hand angered an overwhelming majority of Conservatives along with most voters who call themselves "independent" and even a sizeable portion of Democrats.

For most Americans, including Christians, the idea of having superb health care that is available for all citizens at a reasonable cost is a worthy goal. The objections to the current legislation, however, are many. Protests aren't against the goal of superior health care or reasonable attempts to make that care affordable. The problem is purely in the methodology of achieving that goal. For Christians there is a very strong theological foundation for insisting that the federal government find a different way to tackle the problem.

In an earlier work entitled, *Journey to Unity*, this author addressed the necessary support of a <u>reasonably regulated</u> form of capitalism by Christians. It was pointed out that capitalism, with reasonable restrictions, harnessed the human flaw of greed and directed it appropriately toward the production of successful goods and services. The goods and services that go into a great health care system including health insurance, superior physicians and hospitals can be made better in a capitalistic environment where regulations are aimed at increasing competition rather than controlling prices.

There is no need to recover that ground. While *unrestricted* capitalism cannot be fully supported by Christian theology the idea of completely socializing the delivery of and payment for health care has even less theological support. Doing so removes the necessary profit motive that directs selfish motivations toward fulfilling the needs of the whole society.

Socialization of health care, on the contrary, turns the administration of systems over to individuals who are not restricted by economic penalties if they fail to perform their duties or properly administrate programs. In short, the problems seen in government now (its naive presumption of moral purity in representatives and administrators) will be expanded exponentially. America has already failed to handle this in the Medicare and Medicaid systems which are essentially bankrupt now.

The Republicans in the House voted unanimously against the bill. Prior to coming to the House, the Senate version only gained enough Democrat votes for passage through a series of ugly compromises. These became known as "the Louisiana Purchase and the Nebraska Kickback," where Democratic Senators from Louisiana and Nebraska negotiated unprecedented favors for their respective states in exchange for their votes for the Senate version.

The lack of appropriate decorum in the process was almost universally repugnant to the American people – even among those who supported the outcome. The process itself should be a clear warning that the socialist's agenda excuses all means if the end is considered vital to the cause of limiting the economic liberty of individuals.

The method of passage alone requires Christian support for repeal. If any law is to be passed in America it should have the full force of the democratic process behind it. Anything less than that places America in the same category as impoverished third-world nations run by despotic dictators.

Jesus himself warned his disciples when he asked them, "What does it matter if you gain the whole world but lose your soul?" Winning a legislative victory through deceit and fraudulent means damages the soul of our nation. But what of the goal? Universal health care is certainly an admiral objective to be sure. What would an alternative plan look like if it was constructed by a theologically informed majority of Christian Americans? Let's start first with the goal of having a superior health care system that is available to all citizens. After that, we can look at the methods of insuring and paying for that result.

In terms of comparison America already has one of (if not) the best health care systems in the world. Our medical research is excellent and conducted, for the most part, in a moral fashion consistent with Christianity's view on the sanctity of life. Our nation's ability to cope with delivering adequate care in crisis situations is illustrated by the fact that we not only care for Americans but for a large and growing population of illegal immigrants (at taxpayer expense) as well.

Difficult surgeries are routinely handled and our country's average lifespan has increased over the past several decades. Could America's system of health care delivery be improved? Certainly. There is always room, in a capitalistic economy, for improvement. More importantly there should be a powerful incentive to produce better results under capitalism because whoever outperforms the competition will be able to accumulate more capital. Remember that accumulating capital for investment is the only way new ventures and new jobs are created in the private sector.

Those who favor a socialistic form of health care often criticize the accumulation of capital by asserting that the increased capital is merely going back into the pocket of America's wealthy class. That is not, by any means, true. Profits in health care corporations and drug manufacturers belong to the shareholders and many of those shareholders are everyday people like you. Billions of dollars from our pension plans are invested in those very corporations.

The Christian's theologically based health care agenda, then, should first and foremost include incentives to increase availability of care, incentives to provide that care for less money and incentives to continuously improve the quality of care and service to customers. A capitalistic economy already provides a profit incentive to accomplish all of these ends.

Sick people may not feel great or great about themselves when they are ill but they are customers nonetheless. That means that they are the ultimate arbiter in deciding whether or not the care they receive is worth the money they have to spend for it. If instead of having to pay for their own healthcare the sick person turns that duty over to the State, the sick person is no longer the customer. The State becomes the customer and is completely disassociated from the goods and services received. That interrupts one of the principle benefits of capitalism – customer feedback.

Since the State will have no idea of how well a hospital or doctor performed it will never be able to provide the necessary feedback to assure that quality of care is constantly improving. Worse still, if you have a problem with the service you receive, you won't be able to withhold payment as a means of getting a care provider's attention.

Furthermore, the State will have to ramp up a new bureaucracy just to handle the payments. If that new government entity is anything like the historic growth of other government departments it will continuously grow without actually providing a measureable qualitative difference for the people who become sick. In fact state bureaucracies typically decrease the quality of services for which they pay by arbitrarily deciding what is and what is not a medically required service or treatment. The only means they have to reduce the cost of health care is to simply decide to pay less for what is delivered or reduce the amount of services delivered.

Remember what it was like to go to the doctor when you were a child? Remember how your mother or father sat there in the office with the doctor and tried to understand what was wrong with you and how you were going to get well? Your parents no doubt had your best interest at heart – after all they loved you. Treatments may have been costly but your parents would do anything to make you better.

A poor diagnosis, a poor disposition on the doctor's part, or even a ridiculous wait in the waiting room might motivate them to find you another physician. Don't count on the State watching out for your interest. If anything the State will reward those providers who are willing to work for less regardless of the way you feel when you leave the office.

The single payer system will force doctors to become far less than the professionals they are now and will ultimately open a means (just like with Medicare) for fraudulent providers to get ahead. For the American Christian, our theology demands accountability from professional doctors and that accountability can only remain firm when the sick person or his/her guardians are writing the checks for the service and are able to raise a little hell (something even Christians are allowed to do) when the service is poor. If you really want to see how profoundly different physicians and their staffs will be if the power to pay for services remains with the person receiving the care look at any chiropractic care practice. While it is true that chiropractors do collect insurance payments (for car accidents, etc.) they are nearly wholly dependent on satisfied customers to build their practice.

Here's a personal observation: My chiropractor, Dr. Thomas Cate of Tulsa, Oklahoma is the only physician I've ever visited where his staff made it possible for me or any client to come in at anytime during the day of my appointment and go immediately into a therapy room and receive treatment without waiting on anyone. Oh, and Dr. Cate's list of daily customers (you have to sign in when you come to his office) can amount to 80-100 per day!

My normal appointments with Dr. Cate include face to face time with him for about three to five minutes (when he "adjusts" me). Add up the time a regular M.D. or D.O. spends with you face to face....it isn't that long is it? Here's the best thing: Dr. Cate has become a wealthy man and I'm extremely happy for him. He has earned every cent of his wealth by finding ways to make his health care delivery systems better than anyone else's. Just so the reader knows, Dr. Cate hasn't paid me one cent to mention his excellent service in this book – but I'll bet he buys a few copies – hee hee hee.

Now I can already hear some of you, perhaps a few medical doctors, saying that chiropractors don't have to deal with same fixed costs in doing business. That is very true and I readily admit that. But why is it so much more expensive and risky for a medical doctor to provide services? The list is long and includes these very important items:

1. Medical doctors cost much more to produce. The education costs alone are staggering. Studies show that a typical medical student in the U.S. will spend between $150,000 and $200,000 to complete their education and become a doctor. Students at well-known universities will pay even more.

2. After graduation, medical doctors spend up to four years at essentially low income levels while completing their internships and residencies.

3. Medical doctors and hospitals are subject to far greater government regulation.

4. The cost of malpractice insurance is truly astronomical. A recent survey showed that Pennsylvania is near the average of all U.S. states in the cost of malpractice insurance. There, internal medicine practitioners pay as low as

$6,000 a year (about the cost to finance a BMW for a year) while OB/GYN's can be charged up to about $64,000 per year (that's about twice the median income for a family of four in America).

5. Supply and demand is always part of any calculation of costs in a capitalistic economy. There are not enough qualified physicians practicing medicine in America and the current health legislation is going to drive more of them away from practice. Americans who watch Grey's Anatomy on television will be surprised to learn that an emergency room rarely has a dozen doctors sitting around waiting for an emergency. In many hospitals the emergency room is covered by less than three physicians. So stark is the shortage of available emergency room doctors that interns and residents can make a small fortune working weekends for nearby hospitals in the emergency room. If an aspiring young resident wants to buy a large screen high definition television with 1080p complete with surround sound and even a recliner from which to enjoy it...that's about two weekends of emergency room work.

These are just a few reasons that health care is expensive. There are many more when it comes to considering why hospital stays are ridiculously expensive. What would an American Christian suggest as potential solutions to these problems?

The supply of doctors isn't limited by a lack of demand in America. It is principally limited by the process by which doctors are certified and licensed. First, doctors must attend accredited programs. In order to maintain the revenue generated by training doctors, schools necessarily limit the number of students they accept and the accrediting associations similarly limit the number of universities who are "accredited" to do so.

Accrediting associations are not government entities but private organizations who are staffed by peers in the medical university system. This system developed on its own as major medical schools sought to confirm their excellence by conforming to the expert expectations of their peer universities. As long as these premiere organizations decide what makes a good program and limits those who do, there will always be a shortage of doctors.

Let's not forget some small things as well like text book costs. They really aren't *small* at all.

First year medical students typically have to pay about $1,600 for first-year textbooks. During the ensuing two years they will spend between $600 and $800 per year. By the way, these textbooks are written by professors who are part of the accrediting system and see to it that there are always "newer and improved" versions for each incoming class of medical students. The system itself is one of the reasons medical costs are so high. It is true that doctors ultimately earn a lot of money for their professional expertise. Christians should not care if doctors make money but they should care if the system creating doctors is unnecessarily limiting the number of Americans who can become a physician and compete for their medical expense dollars.

Here's an example to consider: If a city has a shortage of plumbers the price of plumbing will go up and continue until other plumber-entrepreneurs decide to compete for the business. The city can also decide to loosen the requirements for licensing plumbers thereby increasing the number of plumbers able to compete.

The problem with licensing and certifying any trade is that the process supposedly assures the public that the professional is capable and trustworthy. It is only natural for the public to want assurances that a professional can do the job for which they are hired. It is especially true if that professional is a doctor overseeing a person's health. If there were no accreditation or licensing the public would have to discover good doctors through trial and error. That is clearly not acceptable to anyone.

But what if the standards for accrediting and licensing doctors were uniformly set by either state or federal law? If those standards can be met by a small university in the Midwest the graduating physician should have the same credentials as a Stanford graduate. The process of accreditation has to be opened to a wider group of universities and should, perhaps, even be extended to private corporations who are willing to compete for the education dollar. The accreditation should not be left to members of the current medical education "club."

If you have the opportunity to meet and truly get to know a good physician you will eventually hear stories about their internship and residency years. It's a grueling process that has to be endured and the financial struggles they experience are one reason very few doctors feel guilty about the six-figure salaries and incomes they eventually earn. It is not unusual at all for a family practice physician with 10 years of experience to earn up to and beyond $200,000 per year. Specialty surgeons can earn many times that amount. The first four or five years of practice, however, can be just as difficult as any new business venture.

The levels of skill and intelligence required to get through medical school should be rewarded by the free market. So why are doctors treated so poorly in their first four years of practice? Doctors who complete residencies (at very low salaries) do so in order to get admitting privileges to local hospitals. Without that they are unable to earn income from patients they admit to the hospital. Here again, the system is intentionally holding qualified doctors back while they "pay their dues" to the system itself. In order to open the door to greater competition the monopolistic hospital systems have to be broken. Graduating doctors need a level playing field on which to practice their craft.

It goes without saying that any form of income tax is essentially a disincentive to produce goods and services. It is essentially a way to punish productivity even if it is not intended to do so. No one likes to pay income taxes but Americans seem to have accepted them along with the inevitability of death, and strive to earn enough beyond their taxes to have a desirable standard of living. While the fairest system of taxation is something other than the income tax (more on this later) the income tax, as it currently exists, could provide another way to create more doctors if doctors and other medical practitioners were given significant tax cuts during the first four or five years when they are building a new practice.

This is when their costs are higher and when they have the fewest clients. Why not give them tax breaks that allow them to undercut the prices of established practices? There would be nothing wrong with providing substantial tax credits for medical practitioners of all stripes. This would create a further incentive to join the ranks of doctors, nurses, medical practitioners, and other urgent care professionals. America needs more of all of the above and can get more by making it more profitable to become one.

When considering the amount of government regulation on doctors and hospitals the Christian theologian again returns to the power of reasonably regulated capitalism. Regulations cost money for compliance and they require government oversight which all too frequently is asleep at the switch anyway.

It has been said that the government which governs best governs the least. It's a statement in favor of limited or small government. In practice this statement is often used to support the downward delegation of government responsibility to that level of government closest to the problem. In the case of doctors and hospitals, regulation should be something administered as "locally" as possible where the driving desire is to make a community a great place for growing businesses and the new residents they create. Again, competition makes everyone better. There will always be some who think doctors make too much money as it is. Remember, however, that an increase in the supply of doctors will also have the impact of creating more competition and therefore lower medical care pricing. There will always be some who make more than others but that's part of what makes America and capitalism great.

Next is the issue that gets the most political attention – medical malpractice costs. A common talking point from conservatives during the health care debate was "tort reform." "Torts" describe the part of the law covering malfeasance or malpractice. Over the last several decades awards from juries on malpractice suits have made the risk of making a mistake far too expensive for America's own good.

As insurance companies strive to accommodate the possibility of having to pay out such large sums the costs of malpractice insurance for individual doctors has driven the cost of their services well beyond the growth of the economy. Conservatives have sought ways to limit the damages that can be collected from injured parties and have suggested that frivolous lawsuits receive greater scrutiny in the courts. Plaintiffs (those bringing the lawsuit) should be, they say, responsible for paying the defendant's legal fees plus penalties when their case against the doctor or hospital loses or is thrown out.

Naturally lobbying organizations that represent trial attorneys have fought these reforms and have heavily contributed to Democrats who, by and large, support the grievances of plaintiffs viewing them as the more likely group to be harmed by the current system of medical care delivery. The reason trial lawyers fight so hard against the suggested reforms is that limiting the awards in lawsuits will necessarily limit their income. Most trial lawyers work for a percentage of the potential award and can, because of that, completely fund cases they lose out of their own pocket. Plaintiffs who pay nothing for the lawsuit's trial have nothing to lose and everything to gain. Trial lawyers have one of the richest and most powerful lobbying organizations in Washington, D.C.

Currently seven states have limits on "non-economic" damage claims in medical malpractice suits. The question is whether or not the federal government should unify the laws under a federal limit. If it does what should that limit be? It's interesting to note that when considering the damages one should be able to collect from a doctor over a misdiagnosis or perhaps something more severe such as a loss of life or limb, lawyers go to work to build up a value that represents the value of a human life. They consider such things as mental anguish and suffering.

Here's a thought for Christians to consider: Why shouldn't our nation place the same value on an unborn human who, when born and fully matured, will actually produce several million dollars worth of goods and services over their lifetime? Judges and juries do just that when they award plaintiffs for the loss of life or a limb. A woman whose child is lost in delivery due to physician error might, for example, "win" a lawsuit and receive millions of dollars in recompense for a life that was never given the chance to be lived. Pro-life supporters, like most Christians, might ask, "Shouldn't a woman who intentionally aborts a child pay society for its loss?" Just a thought.

Now, back to whether the federal government should set limits on damages that can be collected in malpractice suits. For the Christian this might sound like a simple fix but it has the potential to create just another federal bureaucracy; trial lawyers will no doubt keep that from ever happening regardless of which political party controls the House and Senate. Why not attack this problem with a capitalistic (free market) solution?

One possible market solution can be seen on reruns of the television program, *Gunsmoke*. Galen "doc" Adams, played superbly by the actor, Milburn Stone, was Dodge City's only doctor. He had a kindly way about him but was certainly capable of exhibiting an ornery bedside manner. Still, he was called upon at any hour of the day or night. His character was a composite of our nation's natural trust in all those who served as "country" doctors.

The program gained popularity during a time when America was still captivated by the miracles physicians accomplished on a daily basis. Interestingly, "doc" was never sued for malpractice. That's actually remarkable because it seemed as though he lost more patients than any physician could possibly get away with in our society today. Milburn Stone was a truly skilled actor and was so convincing when he would shake his head, lower his chin to his chest for a moment and then look up at Matt Dillon (played by James Arness) with those really baggy eyes and say, "I'm sorry Matt, I did everything I could..."

Fast forward a bit in time and we have the character, "Bones" the doctor played by DeForest Kelly in the original television series, *Star Trek*. Although the medicine was more advanced than that shown on *Gunsmoke*, who doesn't remember the self deprecating way Kelly delivered his complaining quip, "Damn it, Jim, I'm just a doctor!"

It seems as though America has forgotten that when it all comes down to it, our doctors aren't supermen. They are just as likely to make a mistake as any executive in the board rooms of major corporations and, like those talented executives who rise to the top of their industry, doctors are mostly successful.

In order to bring down medical malpractice costs, and make pricing medical services more comparable to the natural growth (inflation) of all consumer goods and services, there has to be a way to address mistakes without demolishing the reputation and financial security of an otherwise excellent physician. Only in cases where the malfeasance can be shown to be the result of criminal negligence or gross incompetent should a case be brought to our courtrooms.

Other options are already being tested. Pre-treatment arbitration waivers have been used. These agreements bind both patient and physician to a process that circumvents the courts and takes a claim of malpractice to an arbitrator whose decision is final. However, these "arbitrations" often look like, smell like and certainly feel like going to court. They produce the same kind of "us against them" mentality and only modestly limit awards.

Another similar option is the use of a pre-treatment commitment by the patient and doctor to mediation. Mediation is different from arbitration in that it puts both parties in a face to face situation along with legal counsels paid for by the defendant and the defendant's insurer. Settlements do not see the light of day and therefore have no impact on the physician's reputation. Mediation, ostensibly, should remove the possibility of a jury bent on making millionaires out of injury victims while punishing a class of citizens who are mostly guilty of being "rich enough to pay." This system has faults of its own. Some doctor's actions should be made public...and mediators inevitably become prone to seek the simplest solution rather than one that is morally "right."

What would a Christian solution look like? It might make use of both arbitration and mediation. There is one idea that truly fits the Christian worldview. It would, admittedly, require sacrifices from patients and doctors that neither may be willing to make.

The idea is based on the presupposition of *goodwill* on the part of both parties and the biblical mandate to never take a fellow believer to secular court. Christians are instead commanded to settle disputes among believers with the help of the church and its leadership. But whether a doctor or patient is a professing Christian or not this system can still make use of the same principle of "good will" toward all.

The patient expresses goodwill toward the physician in the sense that the patient has properly vetted a physician in comparison to other doctors in the community. There exists an understanding between doctor and patient that the doctor's credentials and history of service (as well as testimonials in the community) mark the physician as trustworthy – something the writer and corporate guru, Steven Covey, defines as both capable and competent. The patient and the patient's family select the doctor with the same implicit trust that marked an earlier age in America.

The physician expresses goodwill toward the patient in two ways. The first is an economic expression in the form of discounted fees. Discounts should be commensurate with the reduced malpractice costs the physician, under this plan, would no doubt enjoy along with the understanding that he/she no longer has to practice "defensive medicine" by ordering tests and/or therapies that are, in his/her judgment, too costly for their "marginal" benefit.

The second is a continued commitment to excellent service that includes the same kind of mindset exhibited by doctors in the middle of the 20th century who regularly made house-calls. House calls may no longer be necessary but taking phone calls from weary parents at 3:00 AM and providing internet access for immediate response should be handled with the same spirit.

In order to set this relationship up patients and doctors sign a rock solid agreement precluding nearly all malpractice suits while accepting up front that cases of criminal negligence or gross incompetence alone can be brought to suit in secular court.

An independent arbitrator, however, must determine that the physician was either criminally negligent or grossly incompetent before a lawsuit can be filed. In order to conform to the "spirit" of the biblical mandate the arbitrator must be someone in whom both parties place implicit trust. They should not be an adversary to either and, for practical reasons, should not be either a practicing physician or a practicing trial attorney. Retired professionals from either field, however, would likely make good arbitrators.

In order to be operable, these agreements need to have broad participation so that an insurance company can competently rate the physician's malpractice insurance. That means that physicians will have to convert their entire list of clients and insurers will likely incorporate several practices in order to form a group large enough for competent rating. It's imperative that an arbitrator in this system have financial independence from the patients, the physicians and the insurance companies as individual entities. They must be paid for their service and be able to recoup the costs of maintaining sufficient staff to process initial claims of criminal negligence and/or gross incompetence.

Who, then, should pay the arbitrators? The only fair system is to essentially "tax" all participants equally through an arbitration fee paid in equal amounts by the patient and the physician's practice at each appointment. Fees paid for arbitration should be directly deposited into an escrow account controlled and operated by a publicly certified accounting firm.

Annual salaries for an arbitrator and commensurate staff personnel should be ratified annually and paid by automatic withdrawals from the escrow account. Expenses should be paid monthly, forecasted quarterly and audited annually with management and auditing fees taken by the public accounting firm operating the escrow account. Arbitrators and escrow agents (C.P.A. firms) should be contracted for five-year terms at "stakeholder meetings" where patients and their doctor have an equal voice in the selection of an arbitrator and C.P.A. firm. Including the insurance company in this "vote" would give the doctors and the insurers the opportunity to take advantage of the patients. In essence, the physician and his patients must agree on the arbitrator and accounting firm, up front, every five years.

None of the features of this proposal require government intervention. They do not incentivize attorneys to chase ambulances nor do they allow insurance companies to use legal strategies that thwart payment of damages. In fact, if an arbitrator has deemed that a case merits secular court involvement due to a determination of criminal negligence or gross incompetence, the insurance company would be foolish not to settle the case out of court.

This system will unclog our courts, reduce the cost of malpractice insurance, reconnect the doctor/patient relationship of trust and put unscrupulous trial attorneys out of business. It only requires one thing from the federal government: They must get out of the way by allowing insurance companies to compete in any state from any state in underwriting the policies fostered by this system. Competition from insurance companies will drive this option into reality and it will reduce the cost of malpractice in America.

What about the affordability of health insurance itself? Should health insurance be portable in the sense that a covered patient can take his/her insurance from employer to employer? Should insurers be allowed to consider "pre-existing" conditions when pricing a policy? Who should pay hospitals when they have to treat an indigent patient or perhaps someone who is in the country illegally?

The increase in health insurance premiums is one of the major issues Congress has tried to address in one way or another for the last 50 years. However, the Patient Protection and Affordable Care Act passed by Congress and signed into law on March 23, 2010 did not address the actual cost of health insurance. It did address the availability of health care and health insurance to all Americans but leaving out the most important element of cost containment is one reason most Americans favor repeal of the law.

In an article written by Robert Samuelson in *The American Spectator* on July 19, 2010, Samuelson wrote,

If you want a preview of President Obama's health care "reform," take a look at Massachusetts. In 2006, it enacted a "reform" that became a model for Obama. What's happened since isn't encouraging. The state did the easy part: expanding state-subsidized insurance coverage. It evaded the hard part: controlling costs and ensuring that spending improves people's health. Unfortunately, Obama has done the same.

Later in the his article and referring back to the insurance provided in Massachusetts, Samuelson continued,

In 1990, health spending represented about 16 percent of the state budget, says the Massachusetts Taxpayers Foundation. By

2000, health's share was 22 percent. In 2010, it's 35 percent. About 90 percent of the health spending is Medicaid.

State leaders have proven powerless to control these costs. Facing a tough re-election campaign, Gov. Deval Patrick effectively ordered his insurance commissioner to reject premium increases for small employers (50 workers or less) and individuals -- an unprecedented step. Commissioner Joseph Murphy then disallowed premium increases ranging from 7 percent to 34 percent. The insurers appealed; hearing examiners ruled Murphy's action illegal. Murphy has now settled with one insurer allowing premium increases, he says, of 7 percent to 11 percent. More settlements are expected.

According to the Kaiser Family Foundation; Health Research and Education Trust, the average cost of health insurance for a family of four in 2000 was $6,438 for the year. In 2007 that same figure rose to $12,106 nearly doubling in the intervening seven years. This represents a compounding rate of nearly 10% for those years while the inflation rate for the same period hovered around 3%.

In other words, the cost of health insurance outpaced the economy and continues to do the same now. While the government may force all Americans to buy insurance through its most recent Act, there appears to be nothing stopping the ever increasing costs of health insurance itself.

Health insurance, like any form of insurance, is a means of insuring the individual against the nearly unlimited costs of a catastrophic illness or accident. It works by spreading the costs of all covered care between all the recipients of its coverage. Americans are most familiar with automobile insurance where factors such as the driver's age, history and other factors have an impact on the insured's rate. However, the American system of health insurance has several roadblocks set into place by federal and state governments.

Health insurance companies are not allowed to compete in every state from any state. Furthermore, most policies are provided through a patient's employer meaning that those employers who are not able to become part of a larger group of insured companies (a real problem for small companies) will have higher coverage costs than a much larger company or group of companies.

The greatest benefit of a nationalized insurance program is that all Americans would become part of the largest group ever insured – all Americans. The insurance purchase has become mandatory in the new Act. This means that millions of Americans who might otherwise choose not to purchase coverage (principally young Americans who are rarely ill, rarely have a catastrophic illness and generally have very little expendable income in excess of their needs) will be forced to buy it.

Including millions of young people into the "pool" of insured patients will certainly lower the cost of health insurance for everyone else. However, this "organic" increase in the number of patients covered will only affect premiums once. Nothing else is in the pipeline of changes to hold insurance costs down. The mandate forcing all Americans to buy insurance will also not affect the cost of treating those who simply cannot afford health care.

The government, in order to cover everyone, will have to subsidize those who cannot afford health insurance. That cost is going to continue to plague the federal budget and could force reductions in the services covered by the national health policies. Those illegal immigrants who now receive free care will not be insured in this program but hospitals and emergency rooms will still have to provide them with services. That means that those who are in this country illegally *can* continue to receive free care – although it is only to fair to point out that many illegal immigrants do pay for medical care – it's just done without insurance.

The only way to truly reduce the cost of health insurance is to control the cost of the services that are covered by health insurance, cut or reduce services offered, or restrict the growth of administrative costs and profits insurance companies are "allowed" to collect. None of these measures, however, can have near the impact as allowing insurance companies to freely compete in every state and/or develop groups that provide unique savings to its members.

For example, it could cost much less to cover members in a group that have no significant pre-existing conditions or members, for example, who are non-smokers. While life insurance policies are already cheaper for non-smokers and auto insurance rates are cheaper for drivers who have no tickets or accidents, health insurance will necessarily be more expensive when patients who have pre-existing conditions or are particular vulnerable (the aged) are forced into groups of otherwise healthy members.

For the Christian the solution also has to take into account the impact of dependency. Government interventions that increase dependency on government is never preferred to those actions that foster dependence on God. It may be more expensive to have health insurance as we age or as we experience health issues that are chronic problems. However, most of these problems occur when Americans have aged. Ostensibly that should mean that they have had the opportunity to accumulate capital (in savings) and have reduced living expenses such that health insurance should be affordable.

Providing one health policy for all Americans will necessarily redistribute American wealth. It will force young adults to pay more for health insurance than they would otherwise pay and will likewise force all Americans to pay for health care for those who are in this country illegally. With a bent toward fostering a reasonably restricted capitalistic economy, Christians will not be able to fully back the health insurance program represented by the recently passed Act. Polls already show that Christians are not in the minority in holding this opinion.

Creating a competitive environment where health insurance costs will drop, or at least rise in sync with the growth of the economy, means allowing health insurers to compete on a level playing field and acknowledging that some groups of Americans will simply have higher costs because of pre-existing conditions or age.

Can the Christian support the subsidization of these groups with a direct payment from the government? It could as long as the recipients are given a rational means test to assure that they are truly unable to afford insurance rather than opting to buy a Mercedes instead of a Toyota. The existence of classes in America is not, in and of itself, a problem for Christians. Christians admit that they are not entitled to live at some higher standard simply because others can and do.

Dependency on God for daily provisions, including health care and health insurance, is not something Christians are discouraged from doing. This is not to suggest that Christians should forego insurance coverage in favor of waiting for God to heal them. God can heal anyone but counting on him to do so in all instances is an affront to his Sovereignty. Sometimes God will choose to allow someone to die of their illness. For the Christian this is, after all, the ultimate healing.

The fact that America is now grappling with the aging "Baby Boomer" generation is important to address. Our current system of Medicare and Medicaid serve the elderly in this nation with affordable and subsidized health care. The decision to do so was borne out of legitimate compassion and respect for those who have built the economy ahead of us.

Christian theology supports the compassionate aims of both programs and American Christians acknowledge that reducing Medicare and Medicaid coverage may not be an appropriate political or strategic aim. However, Medicare recipients should be "means tested." It is a foundational ethic within Christianity that one should take responsibility for themselves when they have the means to do so.

The Economy and Jobs

While capitalism serves humanity best because of mankind's flawed nature, a completely unrestricted capitalism would lead to desperate poverty for some. There is a role for the federal government in properly regulating capitalism. Its aim, however, should always be to keep the doors of opportunity open for everyone in America to accumulate capital.

From boardrooms to rooming houses, Americans need to retain the power of capital accumulation in order to advance their lives and enjoy their liberties. The American economic history is covered in other works by more proficient writers. However, there is no debate that capitalism is so powerful that it can also create an environment where especially destructive motivations temporarily oppress some.

Notice that the oppression is temporary and comes from destructive motivations – something capitalism is uniquely suited to eliminate or vigorously redirect. Whether speaking of capitalism or socialism, each one is a morally neutral system. We will always have members of the human race that seek self-gratification so singly that they are willing to trample the rights of others. In most societies this is rightly called "crime." Its purveyors are criminals. One system, capitalism, punishes those who become too greedy because their selfishness becomes the sword upon which they eventually fall. Whenever an entrepreneur loses sight of the requirement to produce successful goods and services, the customer rather than the government will kill his/her business.

For the past hundred years of American history our government has somehow lost sight of that fact. It has failed to punish crime and criminals and opted instead to attempt to regulate natural capitalistic development to foreclose the possibility of abuse. What have we learned?

The fact is that humanity's flawed nature is most evident in this very economic history. Humans are really creative. Whenever a barrier is placed in front of humanity it finds a way around or through the roadblock. Just so, regulations in our economy have always been circumvented. As government seeks to regulate one part of the economy unintended consequences rapidly emerge. It may have seemed like a great idea to make home ownership affordable for more Americans. However, regulating the banking system and then using it to force banks to make loans to

Americans who were simply unable to pay for them led us into the mortgage crisis.

Predictably the pundits and journalists in America searched for the evil culprit in this development. Democrats blamed the corruption of the banks, lenders, and even Wall Street firms who invented a new kind of financial trading device called the "derivative."

Derivatives are nothing more than a way to protect a bank or financial institution against the possibility of massive defaults. The seller of the derivative is "betting" that the blocks of mortgages purchased by Fannie Mae and Freddie Mac would not default. The buyers of the derivatives were hoping their loan portfolios would be profitable but wanted to have someone other than the government on the hook if the loans ultimately failed.

Was it "evil" to invent and trade derivatives? More likely it was "evil" to force the taxpayer, through government guarantees on these loans, to back the loans against a catastrophic default and then coerce banks to make loans on questionable terms in the first place. The problem is that "evil" exist in this world and is an equal opportunity sickness. There are some forms of regulation that have genuinely helped build this country. Were it not for the regulation of utility companies rural areas of America might still have no electrical service.

Republicans have owned the "small government," "less economic restriction" platform in this nation for several decades. For the most part they have sought to let capitalism do its thing in fostering economic growth and job creation. While they have fought to keep over-regulation out of our financial markets (and taken the heat for being against the "little guy") they have doubled the error of their Democrat counterparts by continuing to spend America's treasure on programs and projects that should have been left to the enterprising genius of the private sector.

There have been competing ideas on economic theory for a long time. The theories are supported by laboratory evidence alone because no one is really able to properly gauge economic behavior at the micro-economic level. People are simply too unpredictable. However, at the macro-economic level, where general policies are put into effect, there are measureable results from the broader economy that politicians use to support their political agendas. There are two fundamental ideas about how to foster economic growth and its benefit of job creation. They are not hard to understand and any American can see the impact of the two competing ideas with their very own eyes.

Democrats have generally favored Keynesian (pronounced Cane-see-un) economic theory developed by the British economist, John Maynard Keynes, and published in 1936. This theory is often called "demand-side" economics because it posits that a federal government can spur economic growth through government spending. Government spending on programs that support infrastructure or social improvement create demand by forcing construction and development where it might otherwise not be promoted by the private sector of the economy. There are risks involved with this policy because increases in government spending either increase the nation's debt or require additional taxation to fund the spending.

Republicans, on the other hand, are famous for their version of economic theory that was trumpeted by Ronald Reagan's "unofficial advisor" and economist, Milton Friedman. It was called "supply-side" economics and was based not on increases in government spending but on substantial tax cuts.

Tax cuts, it was proposed, would put more money into the economy and therefore motivate the creation of greater supplies of goods and services. With more money in their pockets to spend, the American people would, it was theorized, search for goods and services that were once on their wish list. With enough expendable income, people would turn wishes into needs and fuel the creation of more private enterprise.

The reason Americans, as a majority, have not fully adopted either one of these theories is that the laboratory of any experiment has always been contaminated by event variables. What is an event variable? While Reagan was promoting his tax cuts, and the economy did grow, the federal budget was taken into what was then a significant deficit because another one of Reagan's policies was to increase federal spending on defense as he sought to force the Soviet Union to keep pace during the "cold war."

Although taxes were substantially cut, the revenues into the federal government actually increased. Had the nation saved this surplus or even turned more money back to Americans in the form of more tax cuts we would have had a purer laboratory from which to draw conclusions.

Likewise, the current Obama administration is hoping that the "stimulus" packages passed by Congress in late 2009 will prove to create jobs. However the "recession" the President inherited from the Bush Administration and the mortgage crisis inherited from a Democratic-controlled Congress (they failed to provide adequate oversight of the government guaranteed loans) created a situation where government spending to bail out the financial industry enlarged the nation's debt to astronomical levels and the stimulus package did little but increase that debt even more.

Jobs have not been created or even "saved" as the current administration claims. The problem with both of these "theories" is that neither can account for the creative ingenuity of human beings nor their propensity to always act in their own best interest. Attempts to coral capitalism have proved more difficult than pushing water uphill. The biggest problem with capitalism in America is that it has never had a clean laboratory from which to work. Government interventions of all kinds continually thwart its natural ability to correct market problems. The biggest and longest-term intervention of the government into capitalism's natural engine happened in 1913 with the federal income tax.

Think about this with an open mind. Whenever production is taxed capitalism's principal benefit (capital accumulation) is injured. The income tax in America is a constant penalty for doing what Americans want to naturally do – grow their own nest egg. Human beings naturally enter into social groups because they are economically motivated to make their lot better.

The income tax, which took a great deal of effort and disinformation to pass in 1913, created two very bad things for the nation. First, it throttled down an individual's natural drive to accumulate and invest capital in a future of their own choosing. Secondly, and far worse, it gave the federal government the means to socially engineer the lives of Americans using its power to collect a tax on the one thing Americans cherished most – their very life! For human beings, time and physical energy are the ingredients of what we call labor. Labor, in turn, is the singular thing that defines our lives on this planet. It is our only resource.

Since 1913 Congress has progressively demanded more from its citizens, spent every penny sent its way and used its ability to tax production to change the economic and social behavior of the nation's families. The greatest atrocity of the income tax system, however, is that the government spending it supports has given the ruling elite in America the ability to create whole groups of government dependents.

Each program supported by American income taxes fosters a new dependency somewhere in the nation. Not only that, but the government's appetite for revenue has created a mentality among government bureaucrats and representatives that any and all of the nation's private income is available to them for taxation. This attitude is eerily close to slavery. If Americans had to actually write a check to cover their withholding taxes each month they would be astonished at how much of their *life* has been turned over to federal and state governments.

In a "natural" capitalistic economy social groups can and probably will find ways to finance publicly beneficial spending – like paving streets, for example. But by connecting the collection of revenue to a family's production the system itself creates an antagonistic relationship to the economic liberty capitalism is best suited to drive. Instead of taxing production in 1913, America should have taxed consumption instead. Placing a tax on goods and services would have left the choice of "contributing" to the collective pot of social spending in the hands of consumers and would have remained truly voluntary. It would not have created a disincentive to produce because all families would continue to support the buildup of capital in amounts consistent with their own dreams and ambitions.

In a nation where taxes are collected based on consumption rather than production there would be no need to fund a bureaucracy like the I.R.S. There would not be the need to have expensive public accounting firms to complete personal and corporate income taxes. The greatest advantage, however, would be that the federal government would not be able to force behaviors on Americans that suit the political whims of the ruling elite. In fact, the people would have the ability to restrict spending by simply bottling up their expenditures for brief periods to send Congress a signal that spending more than they take in is not "good economic theory."

Without the federal government taxing production, the nation's individuals would be free to conduct business on a personal or corporate level. Capital would flow to the best projects and jobs would be created by the never ending demand for more capital to fuel private economic growth. The system I am describing has never been tried since the industrial revolution. Imagine what this would do for us now in this highly technological age. Imagine what it would be like to go to a bank for a business loan and not have to show the gross income you'd otherwise lose to federal taxation. Imagine a bank that is able to lend money to you because the federal government is not running deficits that force them to loan to the government instead.

Finally, imagine the increase of privately held funds in banks throughout the country if corporations and individuals no longer had to park profits outside of the country in attempts to avoid or diminish income tax obligations to the United States. If the income tax system was abolished, trillions of dollars held in foreign accounts would be able to come back home to America and jobs would come with it! Another benefit of taxing consumption is that one of the motivations of illegal immigration would evaporate. Those in the country illegally would be paying taxes as they live (through spending) just like the rest of us. If you lived in 1913 and was given a choice between these two scenarios, which would you have chosen?

America is currently fighting two wars on international fronts and at least one unrecognized war at home. The nation entered into a war against terrorism immediately after the 9/11 attacks and decided to locate that war in Afghanistan. That nation was known to be harboring three enemies. Al Qaida, the terrorist organization headed by Osama Bin Laden, was thought to be enjoying safe harbor in that country. The mission was to destroy Al Qaida, find and kill Osama Bin Laden, and then eliminate the Taliban.

The Taliban, a quasi-government entity that had taken effective control of Afghanistan, supported the aims of Al Qaida and those terrorist groups loosely aligned with it (principally Hamas and Hezbollah) to forward the causes of radical Islam including threats to the security of Israel. Americans went into combat to remove that government with the intent to support the Northern Alliance. The Alliance was and still is a weakened government of regional warlords that are more favorable to America and at least marginally more compassionate to the Afghan people.

The war in Afghanistan succeeded in removing the Taliban from control but it has failed to find

Bin Laden and has failed to successfully establish the permanence of the Northern Alliance's control of the country. We are still mired in this war and the objective has turned, during the Obama administration, toward nation building – an objective that was beyond the scope of the general war on terror. Even so, President Obama has declared he will begin withdrawing troops from Afghanistan in 2011.

The second international front is, of course, Iraq. Here American and coalition troops responded to George W. Bush's resolve to remove Sadaam Hussein from power after Hussein and his administration continuously circumvented and/or ignored international demands from the United Nations. The demands, in the form of U.N. resolutions, were aimed to allow inspectors into the country to assure that weapons of mass destruction were not being produced there. No fewer than 17 U.N. resolutions were passed but ignored by Hussein.

The Hussein regime was toppled on very short order and he was subsequently tried for war crimes, convicted and hanged. Our troops, as of this writing, remain engaged in supporting the current Iraqi government but the future is anything but certain. President Obama has indicated that American troops will begin a withdrawal from Iraq in 2010 and will have a complete withdrawal by 2012.

Finally, America is fighting, without the help of its military (except 1,200 National Guard troops), a war against illegal immigration from Mexico motivated by the two-fold problem of economic despair in Mexico and the burgeoning drug/gun trade carried out by competing Mexican drug cartels.

These cartels are warring against each other while the Mexican government and its military remain largely irrelevant in the fight. Drugs coming into the United States and consumed by American drug addicts are funding the purchase of American arms, like automatic weapons and explosive devices, which are then used by the cartels to keep the Mexican government at bay. Recently these drug wars have streamed over into America's Border States. In one case a stray bullet entered the county courthouse of a small Texas town across the Mexican border.

These three wars set the backdrop of the discussion American Christians must have in determining the course of action that best fits the Christian worldview. While we must return to each of these wars for specific comment the

Christian must first discover a few theological principles.

The first is the concept of sovereignty – the Sovereignty of God and the sovereignty of nations. You'll notice the use of a capital letter "S" when referring to God's status and the lower case "s" for that of nations. This is intentional and reflects a critical Christian theological concept.

Sovereignty, in terms of God's status, reflects the Christian faith that God is that beyond which nothing greater can be conceived (by humanity). Humanity is limited by its cosmic environment. We are limited in our ability to perceive reality in terms of the four dimensions within which humanity operates. Those are height, width, depth (dimensions of space), and the fourth dimension, time.

We could, theoretically at least, travel to the very end of the cosmos without ever discovering its origin in terms of cause and effect. Theoretical physicists can speculate about the origins of the cosmos, as we know it, but they must introduce concepts beyond what is practically measureable within space and time to postulate what may have been the event that started the cosmos. So far, they have never been able to determine that first cause of what they call the "big bang." Super colliders are now being used by theoretical physicists to help them determine if their theories of "supersymmetry" can determine how the big bang happened. Even if they discover the means by which subatomic particles may have initiated the start of our cosmos they will still have to determine where and how those subatomic particles came into being.

Since God is, by virtue of his defining character, beyond that which he created, he is by theological definition beyond our conception and exists as Sovereign of all that we (part of that creation) can experience.

The sovereignty of nations is a de facto acknowledgment that nations have the right to exist and exercise an authority over the governed as long as the governed grants that nation its consent. In the world today, nations that refuse to acknowledge the same "natural" rights of humanity that we enjoy here in American are, nevertheless, considered sovereign by organizations like the United Nations. It is important, however, for the Christian to understand that as far as theology is concerned, these types of governments are rogue players operating against the will of God even if he has chosen to tolerate their abuses.

Sovereignty for nations is directly tied to the power they require to maintain control. Here, in this country, we continue to rely on a statement found in our Declaration of Independence that was written to separate our nation from the sovereignty of England. That statement was that a nation must be governed by the consent of the governed. The Constitution starts with the words, "We the people..." For Americans sovereignty is first vested in individual citizens. It the result of being endowed with what philosophers call "natural rights," and what Christians call being created with "free will."

America's founding documents first acknowledge that Sovereignty is the right and domain of God who, through his grace, created humanity in his image and, according to the Bible, gave him "dominion" over the earth. Individual humans, through the operation of free will, exercise a lower level of sovereignty over themselves and can, collectively choose to cede a portion of that sovereignty to the nation that guarantees the protection of their natural rights within a world of foreign powers.

For the Christian, sovereignty is appropriated from the authority and dominion of our God. His Sovereignty guarantees our rights of individual sovereignty as humans in whom he has placed a unique entrustment: freedom to self-determination. Scripture teaches that humanity is flawed but we remain free to choose in whom we place our own faith – whether that is in ourselves (humanism) or in the God that is beyond our ability to completely understand.

In either case the decision demands faith. This individual sovereignty, according to America's founding documents, is the only basis upon which a government can effectively govern – that is with the consent of its people.

America, as a nation, opted to form a more perfect union than that from which we emerged. The Monarchy of England and those of other European countries commanded sovereignty without the consent of the governed. They did so using the power of military force and/or despotic action. That God grants humanity free will illustrates the difference between his Sovereignty and that of nations or governments who take power from its citizenry.

All of this demands that the Christian in America fully appreciate the liberty and freedom that our democratic republic affords us. It demands that we refuse to acknowledge or "recognize" those nations whose powers are otherwise derived. To be very clear, individual Christians are free to refuse recognition of foreign powers that take power from their citizens rather than govern with their consent. Our government, through the Presidential power to conduct foreign policy may "recognize" other nations as a diplomatic measure of strategic policy. We, however, must never fail to remember that it is God's Sovereignty that is at stake whenever a nation fails to acknowledge the natural rights of its people. He will judge between those who usurp this right at the expense of his creation.

This is also why our participation in world governing organizations like the United Nations places our nation at an unnecessary risk since our nation's sovereignty cannot be made subservient to any other power without our consent.

Our nation has the consent of its people to act unilaterally among the world of nations. America does not have to achieve the consent of other nations even though it may, at times, be very prudent to do so. Aligning ourselves as a nation with nations of like ilk isn't a bad idea at all. However, if at any point in time our individual freedoms (guaranteed by our Constitution) are threatened by our nation's associations with other nations Americans have every right to protest. Please notice that the word, "revolt" wasn't used. The reason for that will (eventually) be made clear.

American Christians are indeed fortunate to live in this country where our right to freely worship is guaranteed and where our nation (with a few historic exceptions) has guaranteed the individual's right to life, liberty and the pursuit of happiness. Within the context of our history Americans have collectively given a portion of our own sovereignty to the government in order to legitimate its operation as a sovereign nation among other nations. However, Christian theology (evidenced specifically by Paul's letter to the Romans) does not condone the overthrow of a government.

Governments and the powers vested in leader(s) are to be obeyed by Christians. Why? Paul writes this to inform all Christians that God's ultimate Sovereignty is always at work establishing governments and adjudicating the powers of national leaders. Even though America has a democratic republic and will, hopefully, continue to enjoy that right, we are commanded by God to tread around and not through the actions of rebellion. This makes us good citizens in this world and, importantly, confirms another Christian theological truth –

we are citizens of another world where God rules and reigns and forever will do so.

The conduct of foreign policy and the ultimate action of declaring war must be taken with these concepts of sovereignty into account. Here are some thoughts that are consistent with Christian theology:

1. Christians have every right to seek to be governed by a government that recognizes the individual sovereignty given humanity by God by virtue of the free will he gave each and every human being.

2. Christians do not have the right to seek the overthrow of the governments who exercise authority over them. That right has been reserved by God. His actions, as recorded in the biblical account demonstrate that he will supernaturally respond to the oppression of citizens by their governments.

3. The sovereignty granted to governments from those whom they govern is not thereby an authorization to force their national will on other nations whose sovereignty is equally superintended by God.

4. Nations do have the right to protect their citizens against an encroachment

of a people's God-given rights by another nation.

5. Christian theology supports the concept that the earth belongs to God including the resources contained within it. However, that same theology confirms that God granted dominion of the earth to humanity and that the practical application of that dominion should be expressed through national sovereignty rather than through anarchy.

6. American Christians can support cooperation between their own nation and those with whom that nation finds a common acknowledgment of the individual rights God has granted all of humanity.

7. American Christians should not support cooperation between their own nation and those nations who do not acknowledge the Sovereignty of God and/or the natural rights God has granted all of humanity. Alliances of convenience (America's history of considering the enemy of our enemy a friend) are dangerous and threaten the blessings God grants to any nation that acknowledges God and mankind's natural rights which are endowed by him.

8. Christian theology supports the involvement of individuals in the military of their respective nation provided that nation acknowledges the natural rights God has granted all of humanity. Unless conscripted against their will, Christians living in nations that do not acknowledge the individual rights God has granted all of humanity are not obligated to serve in the military.

9. Christian theology demands that a very careful consideration precede any action of war against another nation and that a "just" war include one or several of these conditions:

   a. That nation has first attacked America or Americans. (Like the attack on Pearl Harbor, the 9/11 attacks, or terrorist actions taken against Americans or American soldiers anywhere in the world).

   b. That nation is actively oppressing American citizens through imprisonment or captivity or the elimination of the natural rights God grants all of humanity. (Example: the Iranian hostage crisis)

   c. That nation attacks, threatens to attack or materially harms an

American ally (a nation who, like America, recognizes the rights God grants all of humanity. (Example: German attacks on the nation of England in WWII)

d. That nation attacks or even threatens the security of America, America's allies, or nations whose demise would create instability in a region where government(s) acknowledge the rights God grants to all of humanity. (Example: the development or acquisition of nuclear weapons for the expressed purpose of creating instability or potential use against an a sovereign nation that acknowledges the rights God grants to all of humanity – like Iran's threat to the security of Israel or North Korea's potential threat to South Korea)

e. Nations have the right to put down internal rebellions or civil conflicts from citizens who abuse or fail to acknowledge the rights God grants all of humanity or citizens who, having given their consent to be governed, rebel anyway.

10. The fact that a sovereign nation carries out public policies that are inconsistent with American values or law is not, by itself, justification for exercising diplomatic or military intervention. (Example: America should never have and fortunately didn't conduct a "shooting" war against the Soviet Union although the buildup of its own defenses was certainly justifiable. Diplomatic pressure or blockades conducted against nations who abuse their own populations is not, by itself, justified by Christian theology. A war to free citizens of Somalia from renegade bands and quasi-governments cannot, by itself, be justified. Here Christians must depend on the direct and supernatural intervention of God)

As far as American Christians are concerned, the conduct of America's foreign policy and its prosecution of war should be consistent with the nation's underlying Judeo/Christian theology. It can only remain so if American Christians accept their duty to act together as a majority by electing moral representation in the government. Christians realize that the federal government has to fully consider all options – including those proffered by non-Christian representatives elected by local majorities where Christian influence is not significant. Political parties often differ on issues of diplomacy but have historically coalesced in unity when military action is undertaken.

Likewise, American Christians should commit themselves to the success of our nation's endeavors even when those actions do not align with our own preferences. This is our responsibility toward our nation and exhibits our faith in the Sovereignty of God and his ultimate aim of bringing justice to humanity.

This means there may be times when God's justice is superimposed on America as a sovereign nation. Christian theology, however, does not paint God's character as arbitrary. He is not an impersonal deity bringing earthquakes and pestilences for his own entertainment or to merely vent an uncontrolled anger toward humanity.

The character of God is revealed through the power of his Spirit as individuals and nations encounter him outside the domain of space and time but instead within the existence that humanity can only see through faith. Within the cosmos of faith, spiritual realities supersede those things that are limited to our sentient capacities.

God's justice, as seen through the faith of Christian theology, is redemptive. It was his justice that compelled him to send his only Son to become an atoning sacrifice for the sins of the world. Individual Christians rely on that atonement every day in order to access the grace God provides to forgive and forget our trespasses – even those mistakes we make in granting a nation the right to act on our collective behalf. God's grace also operates outside of time and its limitations that we, as humans, experience. God's forgiveness extends to sins yet uncommitted by individuals and by nations.

At times we must rely on God to address and correct national sins where the accountability for a trespass against God's will is shouldered by the nation's leaders. The founding fathers seemed to have understood this awesome responsibility, too. Actions like the opening prayer before daily sessions in Congress may seem merely "traditional" to our highly secularized society of today. Some have even tried to stop this particular activity through a secularized interpretation of the First Amendment. The Pledge of Allegiance contains the words, "under God" and our currency bears the slogan, "In God we trust." These are echoes from America's past that our foundational precepts acknowledged the Sovereignty of God over the actions of sovereign nations.

Christian theology mandates obedience to those in whom national leadership is entrusted understanding that God himself will judge their actions. In summary, individuals are accountable to God for placing their trust in a nation and the representatives they send to the national government are accountable to the individuals collectively and, importantly, to the Sovereign God from whom the endowment of individual sovereignty comes.

Clearly there must be balance between authority and accountability as it relates to individual sovereignty, the sovereignty of nations and the Sovereignty of God. The liberties that Americans, as individuals, enjoy are part of the inalienable rights God has granted us along with our individual sovereignty – our "free will." Individual sovereignty, then, finds its source in God himself. It includes significant authority to act in one's best interest but an equal responsibility to remain associated with the source of that liberty because it is to God that individuals, in Christian theology, are accountable.

As individuals, Americans entrust our collective sovereignty to our national government so that it governs with the consent of the governed. The leadership that we elect owns the authority that consent implies. As such that leadership is accountable for the nation's actions. In our system of government, the president holds a uniquely ominous accountability for the way in which our nation conducts its foreign policy.

In recognition of this incredible burden our founding fathers made the declaration of war the responsibility of the Congress. This provided a wider group of counsel in determining whether a war was "just" or not. It also absolved individual Americans from the accountability of that decision by placing that accountability squarely on the shoulders of elected leaders. However, this ceding of authority from individuals to what becomes a sovereign nation does not forever absolve the individual from accountability.

Christians are accountable to God for the actions they take to grant a nation its power. Through this accountability individuals must constantly reinforce the truth that the definition of "justice" remains within the

Sovereign domain of God. He is the ultimate Judge and will, at the end of time, judge all the nations of human history and the individuals who, over time immemorial, vested individual authority to those nations.

This concept is vitally important to Christians because there have been and will be future cases where our nation or another in this world will commit an unjust act of war. God does not grant individuals the right to judge a nation nor does he grant individuals the prerogative to judge citizens of a nation that happens to be immorally governed.

In those cases where America is unjustly attacked it should and probably will respond forcefully with the justice of God reinforcing the righteousness of the action. This is only proper and within the national rights it enjoys as a sovereign nation. Is there a limit to a nation's authority to act against another nation that commits an unjust act of war? Is annihilation an option? What of the innocent individuals within that nation who are morally opposed to their government but still subject (under national sovereignty) to it?

The world has entered an age where the response to an attack will nearly always impact innocent civilians. Regardless of attempts to limit "collateral damage," recent history has shown the futility of that objective when terrorist hide within civilian communities and even use women and children as shields when they come out in the light of day. Americans have exhibited anger over the continuous stream of cowardly attacks by terrorist who do not acknowledge those military rules of engagement that have maintained honor between combatants for centuries. In their anger some have suggested that America execute the nuclear option. While this opinion may be openly spoken aloud by a small minority of Americans it is by no means something a majority hasn't at least mentally considered in the heat of the emotional distress after terrorists attacks like those of 9/11.

Christian theology cannot support indiscriminate use of deadly force – even in war. Civilians are called "innocents" for a reason. On the one hand it is true that civilians in a democratic society are responsible for whom they elect to leadership but that accountability is to God himself. In most of the nations where terrorist are harbored, those nations are governed by unelected warlords, despotic monarchs or terrorist infiltrators who use terror to control the local population.

While it is ethically responsible and morally imperative that America develop appropriate military "rules of engagement" for each battlefield, there will never be a "clear battlefield" in the fight against terrorism. As such, America's congressional leaders need to play the part our constitution demands of them and make appropriate declarations of war naming the exact entity or nation at war with America.

Congress must also warn its declared enemies of those conditions in which a largely innocent civilian population will be in harm's way. After doing these things, the leaders of the terrorist organization and/or the governments harboring or supporting terrorists will bear the accountability for civilian losses to God. The only exception, of course, are those losses that are the result of American soldiers operating outside of their own expressed rules of engagement.

If, God forbid, our own nation commits an unjust act of war the accountability for that action will properly remain with our nation's congressional leaders and the President who acts as Commander in Chief of the armed forces. Individual Americans cannot "individually" be accountable but it goes without saying that individual Christians would be under a moral imperative to remove and replace those leaders whose actions were immoral through the electoral or recall process – not through force or rebellion.

Leaders who act unjustly must be punished by their own nation under the authority and responsibility of its national sovereignty. If that nation fails to do so the leaders will ultimately face the judgment of affected nations who suffered from the abuse of power and its attending horror. Ultimately, however, God himself will judge all nations, including the United States.

Based on this discussion American Christians should be prepared to develop specific policies for these difficult issues currently facing our nation in the arena of foreign policy:

Iran's nuclear ambitions and its terrorist connections:

America's history with Iran cannot be ignored but the account is too long to contain in this writing. It is safe merely to say that Iran and America do not speak the same "language" in terms of individual sovereignty and the liberties that a nation's citizens should enjoy as gifts from God. Iran is a nation under the rule of a religion (Islam). Notice the use of the word, "religion" because just as Christian denominations practice a "religion" so do the variant forms of Islam roughly categorized as either Sunni or Shi'a.

Islam's theology, its interpretation of God's role in the universe and man's relationship to God, does not consider humanity's unique position as being made in God's image but flawed by sin. The theology does not provide for salvation in terms of atonement but instead demands belief and acceptance of six fundamental articles of faith.

They are belief in God (the one and only worthy of worship) belief in the prophets, angels, the books (including the Quran), belief in a final judgment and belief in fate. Some of these theological positions are in direct conflict with that of Christianity and Judaism. Islam depends on a continuous stream of revelation embodied in a logical discourse called a dialect that is carried out by its Imams. This process reflects the history of philosophical pursuit that dominated the geographic centers of Islam and the founding of its theology.

Iran's ruling clerics oversee a supposedly secular administration that is elected under conditions that are not remotely "democratic" as Americans understand that word. As the mouthpiece of the nation, its president, Mahmoud Ahmadinejad, has denied the Holocaust and routinely spouts pronouncements of power and intent that are closer to those of a lunatic than a serious statesman. A nuclear Iran is a serious threat to Israel but is it a threat to America?

There are Christians who would argue that any threat to Israel *is* a threat to Christianity. This sentiment is based on the prevailing idea that Christians must support Israel's aims simply because they are the parent nation and religion through which our own theology emerged. A specific reference to Psalms 122 by Christians carries the idea that Christians are obligated to pray for the peace and prosperity of Israel for that act will promote a personal and perhaps a national blessing from God.

Another passage, Genesis 12: 2-3, contains God's promise to Abram (later renamed Abraham) when God called him to leave his homeland in Ur of the Chaldeahs (modern day Iraq). In that promise God states that he will "bless those who bless you (Abraham) and curse those who curse you and all peoples of the earth will be blessed through you."

The second passage contains the specific blessing contained in God's plan to raise a nation that would belong to God. That nation would emerge from the lineage of Abraham through his son, Isaac, and his grandson, Jacob who would go on to have his name changed by God to "Israel." The land that God promised to Abraham contains modern day Israel but that nation's current borders do not reflect the totality of God's Promised Land. If Israel were to occupy the entire Promised Land they would have possession of land in modern day Jordan, Syria, Lebanon and part of the Egyptian Sinai.

Christians understand that the totality of Scripture (both Old and New Testaments) point to a future time when God will supernaturally intervene in Israel's history to reestablish a nation whose ruler will be God himself. This promise is tied to the numerous prophecies concerning a coming Messiah (Savior), born in the lineage of King David, who would conquer Israel's enemies.

Christianity holds the view that Jesus fulfilled part of the prophecies to Israel for the expressed purpose of becoming the sacrificial atonement for humanity's sins. Its theology also declares that, in keeping with the promise of Jesus himself, he will return to completely fulfill the promises of Messiah concerning the nation of Israel and the world as well.

The turmoil Israel faces on a daily basis is part of a long history of conflict between the Arabs (descendents of Abraham's son by the concubine, Hagar) and Israelis (descendents of Abraham through his wife, Sarah). The conflict has, historically, been complicated by the conversion of the Arab nations to Islam – a development that occurred dating from 610 to 630 AD and the life and writings of Islam's prophet, Muhammad.

The conflict was further complicated by the actions of the Catholic Church which, throughout the middle ages, conducted several Crusades under Papal authority to conquer Jerusalem and eliminate Islamic influences throughout the known world. During the Crusades, the Catholic Church operated as a sovereign nation (as it continues to do to this day) and various Popes throughout that time solidified their earthly domains through conquest rather than spiritual conversion.

The current conflict between Islamic nations, (including Iran which is Persian as opposed to Arab), and Israel centers around the post World War II conflicts in Jerusalem and Palestine between Arabs and the Jewish Agency, led by David Ben Gurion (the first Prime Minister of Israel). During the years immediately after the Holocaust and up until the intervention of the allied forces, the Jewish Agency conducted military operations to secure a Jewish State through force. As a complete understanding of the impact of the Holocaust emerged, the existing superpowers developed a sympathetic approach to providing the world's Jews a homeland of their own. The United Nations approved the partition of Palestine in 1947 and events thereafter led to the acceptance of those boundaries and the immediate recognition of Israel by the United States and the Soviet Union.

However, the establishment of the new nation displaced Arab Palestinians who lived inside the nation's new borders. Palestinians with various ethnic backgrounds sought refuge among other Arab nations. Although sympathetic to the plight of Palestinians, the

Arab nations provided little in the way of land for settlement and instead chose to use the action of creating Israel as a rallying point from which to set their theology against that of Judaism. Islam's clerics, in one form or another, have perpetually authorized Jihad (a kind of purifying war) against the State of Israel and subsequently against Israel's supporters as well, including of course the United States.

While American Christians are generally sympathetic to Israel's right to inhabit the land of Palestine, as a divinely ordained action of God, many are equally aware that the conflicts they experience are rooted in a spiritual battle God sovereignly ordained and forecasted in the accounts of both Old and New Testaments. These prophecies indicate that the conflict will not be fully settled until the end of time and will also be preceded by a period Scripture calls the Great Tribulation.

Christian theology supports the claims Israel has to the entire boundaries of the land ceded to Abraham and subsequently occupied by Joshua and the 12 tribes of Israel. The call to pray for and to "bless" the nation is motivated by the faith placed in the sovereign plan of God and his selection of that nation as his own unique instrument in dealing with all of humanity.

This divine selection, however, is also part of God's plan to provide salvation through Jesus, the Messiah, to Israel and the entire human race. The Apostle Paul makes it clear in his letter to the Romans (chapter 11, verse 23) that all of Israel will be saved at the completion of the "times of the Gentiles."

Christian theology could conclude that threats to Israel are, in fact, threats to God's Sovereignty. To do so, however, would be to doubt God's ability to superintend his own possession. After the Six-Day War in 1967, many Christians came to understand that Israel remains under God's protection and that he will indeed fight against her enemies in truly miraculous ways.

Some believe that attacks on Israel will destabilize the region and cut American access to critical resources. In this situation a Congressional declaration of war to both support a loyal ally and protect our access to critical resources could be justified. However, a preemptive action by America against Iran would not pass Christian theological muster. Unless first attacked by Iran or threatened with a clear and present danger to our own national security, any action outside of those to support our alliance with Israel would be theologically unsupportable.

The prophetic documents of Scripture indicate that preemptive actions by any nation either against Israel or even in support of Israel will not deter the fulfillment of God's divinely ordained plan for that nation. While Iran is an international nuisance and could become dangerous with nuclear weapons, her potential actions against Israel will be met by the divine intervention of God himself who, as it happens, has seen to it that Israel is fully capable of its own nuclear response.

North Korea's Nuclear Ambitions:

The foregoing discussion regarding Iran can be partially duplicated here without the historical and theological connections of any hostility toward Israel. In the case of North Korea its hostility is directed toward it neighbor (and common nationals) to the south. America's interests lie exclusively in our support of the democratic regime America helped establish in South Korea. Here is a classic case where America's ongoing interest in South Korea has little to do with that government's place in our national heart.

For the most part South Korea is one of the few successes America has witnessed in the art of nation building. Our efforts there along with those of the South Koreans themselves have established a democratic nation that participates in the global capitalistic economy producing numerous products that make their way back to our own nation.

America's entry into the Korean War was significantly motivated by the cold war dynamics of fighting the spread of communism. North Korea's existence to this day is heavily dependent on the acquiescence of China. The common link between them is communism but North Korea's leadership, like that of Cuba, is literally steeped in an era that passed with the decline of the Soviet Union and the globalization of the Chinese economy. China may not be capitalistic in the sense that its economic system is similar to developed democracies. On the contrary, China continues to support a centrally planned economy but even they have come to the conclusion that national progress is meaningless unless it can keep its billion people happy and moving forward economically. They are rapidly learning what capitalism really does for an economy and their continued support of America through the purchase of American treasury notes (they are financing a large portion of our national debt) evidences that their interest in maintaining North Korea's friendship is moving way down on their list or priorities.

This is the reason for America's decision to hold very public military exercises with South Korea's navy in response to North Korea's sinking of the Cheonan (a South Korean naval ship). For its part, North Korea has rattled its saber and acted like a national three-year-old. If they have acquired nuclear weapons and intend to use them on South Korea, America's response should be forceful in support of our ally there. However, the strength of our presence in South Korea should not replace the resolve of that sovereign nation to defend itself. It would be better if America simply armed South Korea with an equal counterforce to act as a deterrent to the insanity of North Korea's leadership. The onus should be on China to control its orphaned nephew. Meanwhile, the global community of sovereign nations (not the United Nations by the way) should pressure China to rein in this bad actor.

Good theology suggests that America do all that it can to stay out of unnecessary interventions where the nation we are supporting has not exhibited a similar dedication to prudent self defense or diplomatic wisdom. Furthermore, nations that rely too heavily on American intervention have proven, historically, to be just as quick to hate us for that saving grace. America's unique history should be proof positive that the organic growth of capitalism and democracy cannot be replaced by a "white knight" foreign policy.

Illegal immigration from Mexico and the forces behind it:

Illegal immigration into the United States has been a problem for decades leading up to the current crisis of confidence that inspired the Arizona legislature to pass, and Governor Anne Brewer to sign into law, one of the nation's most controversial attempts to curb illegal immigration within a Border State. Increases in violent crime and the costs borne by Arizona for law enforcement and social services provided for illegal immigrants was just part of the motivation behind the law. The law, now understood to be essentially a duplicate of existing federal immigration law, empowered State law enforcement officials to inquire into the immigration status of persons they encounter through normal lawful stops if, during that process, they develop reasonable suspicion that the person in question is in the country illegally. The law specifically prohibits racial profiling in the development of reasonable suspicion.

Frustrated over the federal government's failure to enforce its own laws, the Arizona legislature, at the expense of the State, opted to beef up the enforcement of federal law with local police and sheriff department assets. Persons stopped in the course of criminal activity or traffic violations that are determined to be in the country illegally are, according to the State's new law, turned over to federal authorities with the Immigration and Customs Enforcement agency (ICE).

The Obama administration's response to this law was to falsely claim that the law was racially motivated and that it would result in racial profiling. This position was picked up by the main-stream media as though it were fact. The Arizona law, a document covering about 16 pages, was apparently not read by members of the media. This is significant because statements (made by Eric Holder, the nation's Attorney General and Janet Napolitano, the United States Secretary of Homeland Defense) were made prior to either government official actually reading the law. Both openly admitted this before congressional committees or in responses to questions from the press.

The Obama administration's disinformation inflamed the anger of legal Hispanics and other potentially affected minorities as they surmised that lawful stops in Arizona would be arbitrary and motivated by racial appearance only. Politicians on the right mainly viewed the disinformation as an attempt to drive attention to the administration's central policy on immigration from Mexico – a policy called "comprehensive reform" which would ostensibly embody solutions to all of the problems contributing to the causes of Mexican citizens illegally entering the United States.

During the Reagan administration the problem was addressed through a similar "comprehensive" approach that ultimately failed to produce acceptable results. An estimated three million illegal immigrants already in the country at that time were granted amnesty and a relatively easy pathway to citizenship. Today it is estimated that between 12 and 20 million persons are in the United States illegally. More than 50% are from Mexico and about 25% come for other Latin American countries.

The problems with illegal immigration are profoundly affecting the United States economy as all persons within the United States, legally here or not, are provided emergency health care on demand regardless of whether they can pay for those services. The potential displacement of American workers is often raised as a problem but many will protest that assumption believing that illegal immigrants generally perform work that Americans refuse to accept.

The problem is both a domestic crisis (more States are considering following Arizona's lead) and a foreign policy issue. The Obama administration, after finally reading and reviewing the law, chose to challenge it in Federal Court realizing that it would potentially have to go to the Supreme Court for final settlement. However, instead of challenging the law's constitutionality on the basis of its alleged violations of civil rights, the Attorney General filed suit on the basis that Arizona's law usurps federal authority to set and enforce immigration policy.

In the face of increasing criminal activity along the border and the Mexican government's inability or lack of motivation to curb that activity, a majority of Americans believe the federal government's first priority ought to be to secure the border from further illegal immigration first and then focus on the problems arising from those persons already here illegally.

There is not a strong sentiment among Americans that those who are here illegally should be granted a path to citizenship that doesn't first send them back to their homeland to wait in line for visas as all other legal immigrants have done for more than 100 years.

While the issue of open disobedience to our law is enough evidence for American Christians to favor securing the border on moral grounds, the issue of what to do about the root causes of the flow across our border must be seriously evaluated at some point in the very near future. It is clear that the United States economy represents an opportunity for capital accumulation that simply is not available in Mexico. This is especially true if illegal immigrants are able to avoid paying payroll or income taxes in the process of working here. There are existing laws forbidding U.S. companies from hiring illegal immigrants and the penalties for doing so can be severe. However, the enforcement of those laws is lax at best and completely negligible in a worst-case scenario.

Then there is the problem of the Mexican drug cartels smuggling drugs into this country using illegal aliens as "mules." In addition to smuggling drugs into our country the drug cartels are often collecting payment from illegal immigrants in return for their protection using armed, non-uniformed, combatants. Drugs that fuel American addicts also support the funding that, in turn, is used to project the power of the cartels within the increasingly corrupt Mexican government.

Recently the Mexican government has been pressured into properly policing its border but doing so, in many cases, creates extreme violence between the cartels and Mexican federal police and/or military soldiers sent to enforce the law.

Consider this account from the Associated Press dated July 22, 2010, Nuevo Laredo, MX:

> Late-night gun battles with gangs who forced citizens from their cars and used the vehicles to block streets paralyzed a border city, sound of gunfire alarmed Texans on the U.S. side of the Rio Grande.
>
> The Nuevo Laredo city government posted messages on Facebook warning citizens to stay indoors as the battles erupted at several intersections in the city across from Laredo, Texas...
>
> Nuevo Laredo is among several northern cities under siege from a turf battle between the Gulf cartel and its former enforcers, the Zetas gang of hit men. Violence has surged along the northeastern border with the United States since the two gangs split earlier this year.
>
> Gangs have frequently blocked streets in the middle of the cities to thwart soldiers coming to the aid of colleagues under fire.
>
> In the northern state of Chihuahua, a banner appeared on a bridge threatening violence against "innocents" unless the state government fires its chief of police intelligence, Fernando Ornelas, the Diario de Juarez newspaper reported Thursday.

The banner appeared in the state capital, also called Chihuahua.

Last week, drug gangs introduced a new threat to Mexico's drug war, detonating their first successful car bomb. The attack killed a federal police officer and two others in Ciudad Juarez, Chihuahua's largest city.

Mexico has fought internal corruption for many generations and has never risen to its potential in terms of economic and political stability. The nation has endured extreme poverty and extreme wealth as chronic corruption has eroded the opportunity to grow a functioning middle class. The drift of its citizens to the opportunities in America is understandable but is, nonetheless, a serious problem if that opportunity is being seized illegally. America is a nation of laws and the nation has a right to expect the federal government to completely perform its duty in protecting our borders and enforcing the immigration laws already on our books.

There are those in America who suggest that the Obama administration sees the growing population of illegal immigrants as potential voters dedicated to the Democrat party if through Obama's "comprehensive immigration reform" they should succeed in their efforts to gain citizenship without serious penalty. The Democrat party already enjoys wide support from many minority groups in America and this fact has caused Republicans to turn a jaundiced eye toward the Obama administration's lackluster performance of its duty to defend our nation's border. However, even in the best scenario, current illegal immigrants would not likely gain citizenship or voting rights before President Obama has either succeeded or failed to win a second term.

For Christians the heartfelt empathy for our neighbors is strong. We worship with Hispanics in churches across the country and the population of Mexico strongly identifies with Christianity's Catholic Church. The contribution of traditional Mexican values like the maintenance of strong family units would positively affect the United States and encourage other Christian communities struggling to do the same.

While developing a temporary worker's system that maintains a fully documented stay and return to Mexico can help both country's economies, Mexico must first get control of and prosecute its drug cartels in cooperation with the United States and the country must show good faith toward developing an economic structure within the country that supports the God-given natural rights of all of its citizens. This is one area of our nation's foreign policy that demands Christian involvement. We must seek to generate goodwill toward Mexico while maintaining just laws and obedience to those laws here in America.

For the present, however, American Christians should not support an administration policy that fails to recognize the danger of our porous border nor should it allow the nation's leaders to continually "kick the can down the road" by failing to address the issues that are contributing to the flood of illegal immigrants that depress our own economic growth. Christians need to support actions that make the Mexican government accountable for its own failures while acknowledging that a failed economy in Mexico will always pose a clear and present danger to Americans.

It has to be acknowledged that a desperately failing economy in any one of our States would have a serious impact on any other States on its border. Just by way of example consider the impact the entire Western U.S. would feel if California was to actually go bankrupt – a prospect that is not inconceivable.

While Mexicans speak a different language than Americans, we both speak the international language of economics and both countries have a solid foundation of common and deeply held spiritual values. The best solution for our hemisphere *could* be for the United States and Mexico to bi-laterally chart a long-term (30 to 50-year) path to sovereign unification of our two nations. That, however, could only happen through both countries' ballot boxes.

If that were to happen, there would have to be a generous extension of time to provide both major political parties in this country the time needed to present their competing agendas to a future block of the United States' electorate and to establish appropriate policies that protect the integrity of the American electoral system. The time would also allow Mexico, with America's help, to establish a consistent and sustainable economy that builds a truly representative middle class.

Mexico will never rise above its internal corruption until a capable and incorruptible police force can support the rule of law, and until a civilian leadership can establish a working capitalistic economy. If and when that happens, the United States might be wise to invite Mexico into the family of Statehood.

Participation in the United Nations:

By this time, as a reader, you are probably beginning to compose your own ideas about several of America's pressing foreign policy issues and you are framing them within the Christian theology that elevates the Sovereignty of God to its proper place. You no doubt are also beginning to fully appreciate the majestic gift of the individual's natural rights that are part of God's endowment to all of humanity in the form of free will or individual sovereignty.

Since individuals can and do essentially delegate parts and pieces of their individual sovereignty to a nation in order to establish a national sovereignty as is done here in America through the ballot box, the question concerning the United Nations is where does it derive its authority? Does the United Nations have some form of sovereignty of its own?

The past 50 years has illustrated the impotence of the United Nations to act as a sovereign ruling body and we, as American Christians, should be very happy about that. The fact is that this group of nations has no authority except that which has been delegated to it by the sovereign nations making up its composition. While it is true that our nation's Constitution provides the President with the power to conduct foreign policy and that our Presidents have historically placed their own appointed ambassador to this body, the American people have never had the opportunity to cast a direct vote on its existence and the only action taken by Congress was its action to invite the international group to reside in New York. The United Nations exists apart from any American Constitutional authority. Accordingly, American Christians do not have to accept this group's power nor recognize it as a legitimate sovereign.

The organization itself is essentially undemocratic as well. The existence of the U.N. Security Council, a group of 15 nations composed of five permanent members and ten non-permanent members has the responsibility for world peacekeeping. Policy decisions within this body require a majority vote consisting of at least nine members but any one of the five permanent members has the power to veto a resolution. Additionally, all proposals from the member nations must be routed through the U.N. Security Council. Fortunately, for American Christians, the United States is one of the five permanent members of this body.

However, the continued impotence of the United Nations is caused by the inability of the five permanent members to fundamentally agree on the theological basis of self-government within nations. Apart from that there will never be a true authority and accountability balance from which to properly rule. The idea of having a place for nations to conduct foreign policy in conjunction with other nations sounds great on paper. But paper is just about all the organization has ever contributed to world peace. It is riddled with corruption – even within those organs that have been established to provide disaster relief and aid to impoverished nations.

Watching the operations of the United Nations whenever a major speech is delivered is very instructive for the American Christian. One can't help but notice the funny earpieces worn by the diplomats as they tune into their very own interpreter who hopefully translates speeches accurately. This mental picture should conjure up the story of the tower of Babel from the Old Testament. In that story, the human population has grown exponentially but a large group decides to settle in a fertile area where they build a great tower to the sky. The tower is a sign to potential enemies of their strength but it also becomes an icon for their failure to acknowledge the Sovereignty of God.

From God's perspective (again, outside of space and time) he notices this action and muses to himself that humanity, with a common language and a common intention can, in fact, accomplish anything they desire (within space and time). In order to establish his Preeminence and Sovereignty and to remind the creatures he created that they are, after all, creatures, God confuses their languages so that everyone's communication becomes babble.

The language barrier forces the people to disband and reunite with others who do speak the same language and thereafter life on the planet continues – perhaps with a greater appreciation for God's ability to intervene in human affairs. The point here is that it is the acknowledgment of God's Sovereignty alone that can and eventually will unite the nations of the world. Since it is otherwise impossible to do so, the work of the United Nations is essentially moot.

The moral lesson of the tower of Babel is especially relevant in our world today. Language remains a barrier but the fact is that our technology overcomes that barrier and the vast populations that speak through interpreters have advanced in discoveries and inventions to the point where humanity once again fulfills God's observation. Within space and time humanity is capable of achieving almost anything it can conceive. Like the people of Babel there exists a sort of arrogance toward God that is evidenced in the humanism that competes with the Christian theological position.

Our own history in just the past 20 years shows that the United Nations cannot address the problems of the world as well as sovereign nations acting under the delegated power and authority of its individual citizens. Although President George H. Bush was able to cobble together quite a coalition of nations to drive Sadaam Hussein from Kuwait, no one doubted that the power of the United States was all that was needed to bring that result into reality. The other nations provided the U.S. with "cover" and ostensibly legitimated the action as a "just" war. As Iraq has continued to be a difficult nation to rebuild the blame for its problems is uniformly placed on America rather than on the United Nations or the several partners who have given support to the cause.

This subject has been saved for last in this section because all of the preceding discussion has properly plowed the soil for sowing a fresh look at this old topic. Terror is an emotion that no human being anticipates. It is shocking. The fear it evokes is intended to gradually diminish the resolve of its targets. It has been a successful tool if one grants that terrorism has shaped international behavior for most of the past three decades.

Our lives in America have been severely impacted by terrorism. We have lost friends and loved ones including prominent leaders and courageous soldiers. Travel is not the adventure it once was but has become a tedious nightmare and the terrorist in the world gloat over the massive expenditures America has made to protect our population and our infrastructure.

When George W. Bush announced that America was going to fight a war against terrorism he warned the nation that doing so would not be like any previous war. He spoke of the fact that terrorist hide within civilian populations and noted that some nations behaving as an axis of evil would harbor terrorist organizations. He warned those nations that did so that American forces would count them as enemies as well.

He named a few nations but, as this decade approaches an end, many more nations have appeared to be hiding terrorist and terrorist sympathizers. On July 27, 2010 America awoke to learn of another critical leak of secret documents. Wikileaks, an internet whistle-blower site, received and posted excerpts from over 90,000 classified documents containing reports of action in Afghanistan since 2004.

Long held suspicions were confirmed. For years it has been rumored that members of the Pakistani government were sympathetic to and potentially assisting members of Al Qaida and the Taliban. In fact, members of Pakistan's intelligence service appear to have taken American money to support operations against Al Qaida but have instead covertly supported the group even to the point of helping them plot strategy against coalition forces.

The problem with our war on terror is that it has escaped the normal Congressional inspection and deliberation of a declared war. Lacking an identifiable enemy America, under the authority of our President, chose to attack terrorism wherever it raised its ugly head. Nation States were not the enemy. Instead international criminals, posing as heads of an ethereal State, plotted their crimes from within safe havens either protected by remote geography or complicit national governments.

Christian theology supports the demolition of terrorism as a tool for political aims. It supports the taking of terrorists' lives as just punishment for abhorrent homicidal crimes. But Christian theology also demands much of any nation who, acting sovereignly (with or without their people's consent) aids and abets a terrorist organization. Even those governments that do not support terrorism but find parts of their geographic domain topologically suitable for hiding terrorists have a responsibility to all other sovereign nations to eradicate terrorist from their land and terrorism from their hearts and minds.

A military action against a sovereign nation must first vault the hurdle of a "just" war. What happens when a nation has a "just" cause but no nation on whom to declare war? If terrorist are hiding in Afghanistan, Pakistan, Yemen, Lebanon and Syria, should America declare war on all of those nations?

For the Christian in America there should not be a distinction between nations that harbor terrorists and the terrorists themselves.

Nations who derive their just powers from the consent of the governed have a responsibility to their own citizens to first protect them against terrorist who commit crimes against humanity and second against the military attack from nations who are justly at war with their nation because of its harboring international criminals. Governments have the accountability to arrest and prosecute terrorists regardless of their political or religious affinity with the aims of the terrorist organization. Since they own this accountability they also must be accountable for the state of war that exists between them and America when America is victimized by the terrorist organizations hiding beneath their skirts.

George W. Bush must have been under enormous pressure to act and act quickly once the nation had recovered from the terrible losses of 9/11. In his haste to do something he failed to demand that Congress declare that a state of war existed between America and the nations we knew were harboring terrorist.

Declaring that a "state of war exist" between America and another nation enables the President to prosecute the war with the aim to win decisively and to use whatever strategies and tactics that fall within the moral mandates for which America stands. It is not, however, a moral mandate to avoid civilian casualties in a declared war. The responsibility for civilian casualties when a state of war exists between two nations remains with the civilians' own nation. A country is always accountable for protecting its citizens and that sometimes means warning them that they are going to be in harm's way and sometimes it means building bomb shelters and practicing blackouts as was done in World War II England.

When Congress declares that a state of war exists between America and a terrorist-supporting nation, the President is free to prosecute the war on timing that is beneficial to our own military and completely secret inasmuch as our military can execute a secret war strategy. Afghanistan – even though governed at the time by the Taliban – had the right to know that its nation was in a state of war with America. It deserved ample time to remove citizens from sensitive locations and it deserved time to arrests the terrorist and sue for peace with our nation before we began "killing people and breaking things" (attribution to Rush Limbaugh on the purpose of war).

Had the Afghanistan government failed to turn over the terrorist (and they no doubt would have chosen not to do so) America would have been morally free to prosecute the war with everything suitable in our arsenal to assure a quick and total victory. It may not be diplomatically comfortable but the only way to wage a just war on terrorism is to ask Congress to declare that a state of war exists between America and every nation that currently harbors terrorists. Today that list would include Afghanistan, Iran, Pakistan, North Korea, Syria, Lebanon and Yemen.

Would America have to send troops to all these places at once? We would not and furthermore we would hold the cards as to when and where our military might strike the next blow. The threat of nuclear annihilation might be enough to force these rogue nations into submission. It is not even remotely believable however if our nation's Congress doesn't even acknowledge that a state of war exists.

Americans became weary of the war in Viet Nam and have grown weary of the war on terror. The reason is that America did not win the Viet Nam war (undeclared, by the way) and haven't yet won the war in Afghanistan. Winning a war doesn't take a decade. But fighting around the sensitivities of world opinion and fighting a war at home with a Congress that can withhold military funding can make any war last as long as there is something for one political party to gain at the expense of the other. Our most recent wars amassed thousands of graves for soldiers who, in the end, died because Congress lacked the courage to fight and win a declared war.

Terrorism must be demoralized in order to be defeated. In order to demoralize terrorists a nation has to kill them wherever they live and breathe. If they are hiding behind children it is not the duty of our military to shoot around the innocent to hit the coward behind. The death of innocents in war is on the head of the terrorist organization and the sovereign governments who have failed to keep them out.

The human cost of terrorism is outrageous. Suicide bombings and attacks on innocent citizens can only be stopped when a sovereign nation, acting by the consent of the governed, moves with courageous conviction that they are fighting a just war. In so doing that nation is acting in congruence with the Sovereign will of the Creator who endowed all humanity with natural rights including the right to exist free from terror.

From his position beyond space and time God will judge the intentions and actions of nations. Christian theology understands that God is gracious and will forgive nations who take human lives in the prosecution of wars against those who ignore the natural rights of men, the sovereignty of nations and the Sovereignty of God himself when they commit acts of terrorism.

Separation of Powers – *The Presidency*

Every year American presidents make the trip over to the United States' House of Representatives to make a formal address to the nation. This address is made during television's prime time and is covered by most major broadcast and cable networks. The event is attended by representatives from all branches of the federal government even though the event is certainly not compulsory. Members of the Supreme Court, both houses of Congress and key groups like the military and Foreign Service are also represented.

The speech is measured, in part, by the number of interruptions for applause a president receives and journalists often evaluate the effectiveness of the speech with this measure. Of course Americans have become accustomed to watching the drama and, for the most part, discounting the impact of applause noting that the President generally receives the greatest response from his own party. Likewise, the thunderous silence of the opposition party often raises our collective attention to the degree to which the two major parties in America have become exaggerated caricatures of their original charters.

During the last State of the Union Address, President Obama broke a long-held tradition when he directly criticized an entire branch of the government. It is not uncommon for a president to criticize the opposition party's policy or to promote his/her own with intensity. In this case, however, the President responded to the Supreme Court's decision to strike down critical portions of the McCain/Feingold Campaign Finance Law. In a narrow 5-4 decision, the Court ruled that the Federal Government cannot ban political spending by corporations.

This open breech between one branch of the government and another excited journalists and alarmed citizens because it indicated that the President questioned the very fabric of our Constitution's check and balance system. Chief Justice, John Roberts, had to respond and chose to do so with as much decorum as he could muster. While addressing a group shortly after the speech, Roberts was asked whether he felt the venue of the criticism (the State of The Union Address) was appropriate. Roberts answered, "...there is the issue of the setting, the circumstances and the decorum. The image of having the members of one branch of government standing up, literally surrounding the Supreme Court, cheering and hollering while the court -- according the requirements of protocol -- has to sit there expressionless, I think is very troubling."

The use of major media events like the State of the Union Address to impact American opinion certainly isn't new and President Obama did not invent the tactic. While the majority of Presidential addresses to the nation have never been televised, the event took on a whole new meaning during the Reagan administration. Reagan was, without a doubt, the most professionally skilled communicator to occupy the office up to the time of his inauguration. As a former Hollywood actor, he was not only accustomed to the camera but was aware of the cinematic strength of storytelling. He was the first president to invite special guests to the event where they traditionally sat near or even next to the President's wife, Nancy Reagan. At some point during his speech, Reagan would call attention to the person and tell their story – generally a story that illustrated the strength of Reagan's policies.

This drama was immediately absorbed by Americans who, sitting in their living rooms, suddenly sat forward in their easy-chairs to hear about one of their own. The event ratcheted up the expectation for entertaining drama during the speech. Reagan continued to deliver with speeches and drama that captivated the nation and led to his famed moniker, "The Great Communicator." On the other hand, the continuation of that drama by lesser lights in the oval office has served to progressively denigrate the overall effect. The event has turned into a populist ceremony that often looks more like a campaign event rather than a serious evaluation of our democratic republic. In turn, the transformation of what was once intended to be a patriotic rallying point for all Americans has become just one more place for party politics to separate citizens.

The point is that Americans have become disconnected from the intent of our Constitution where presidents, regardless of party affiliation, accepted the responsibility and accountability to address the entire government (along with the American people) explaining in simple terms the condition of the nation among the nations of the world and the condition of the citizenry within the republic. While it has historically been appropriate for Presidents to lay out their agenda for the upcoming year, that agenda was traditionally set within the framework of encouraging the protection of the American dream for all citizens inviting the cooperation of all government branches.

This discussion's aim is to remind Americans of what once was the role of the President. Our nation will forever have only one "First President" in George Washington; perhaps the greatest tragedy is that America's founding fathers chose to ignore one of his most prescient pieces of advice. Washington hated what he saw in the trend among his peers to create political factions within the government. As he predicted, the nation immediately began to fracture into political parties signaling something that he alone seemed to see as a danger. It was not the danger of dissention but the impact of dissention on the <u>Office</u> of the Presidency.

While the Constitution certainly does not forbid the establishment of political parties, Washington saw the grave consequences of future Presidents beholden to the parties that elected them. He was elected our first President on the strength of his non-partisan service to our nation as its military leader and "conqueror" of the English "Red Coats." As a civilian Washington began to see, first hand, how divided loyalties within the nation could cripple the executive branch of government.

The crippling effect has never been more evident than today.

The Constitutional establishment of a bi-cameral (two houses) form of Congressional representation allows the nation to hear competing versions of where we are and where we are going. The rise of party politics within these two houses of the legislative branch is not a threat to the nation but should continue to be one of its strengths. While the decorum of the legislative branch is strictly enforced to this day there remains a vibrant dialogue among our representatives that anyone can watch by tuning into C-Span. The raucous style of debate seen in the English Parliament makes our nation's Congress seem tame by comparison. It is within our House and Senate that ideas form and either gain support or fade away.

As the nation's population grows and evolves political parties seek to hold majorities that can help them affect change consistent with their own view of governance. Ideas about economics and policy either get traction in the legislature or go back to party drawing boards for reconsideration and amendment. This process naturally involves the electorate and American citizens have learned that their power at the polling booth is not insignificant. In terms of how this impacts the duties of the

President, however, has been largely missed because no one can recall anything other than what we have experienced for many generations.

The way America's presidents were first elected left the American voting population completely out of the process. Each State was assigned a number of "electors" based on the total number of the State's delegation to Congress. These electors were authorized to cast two votes each for the President. They were not, however, allowed to cast both for the same man or to cast them for two men from the same State. If no person received a majority of the vote, the top five were then sent to the House of Representatives where the President would be elected. The only requirement was that the President elect had to receive majorities from a majority of the States' delegations to the House.

This process was eventually changed by the twelfth amendment which created the Electoral College and turned over the vote for specific electors to the American people. Many Americans to this day don't quite understand the Electoral College. In essence, we the people do not actually vote for the President. We continue to vote for "electors" who are honor bound (in some cases legally bound by State law) to vote for the presidential candidate supported by the majority of the elector's State. This change forever made the office of the President a political position requiring significant support from the political parties from which they emerged as candidates and for whom they necessarily owed allegiance. Prior to this change the President enjoyed a modicum of separation from the sometimes "dirty" work of political factionalism.

It is entirely possible that this change has also hampered the development of a consistent national character when it comes to addressing the nation's problems. As the "Chief Executive" of America's executive branch of government, the President must execute the laws duly passed by Congress. He/she must propose an annual budget to Congress but it is the responsibility of Congress to pass a budget and to make appropriations (expenditure decisions) consistent with that budget. Once the budget is passed, the President has the authority to execute the budget and, through the power of the executive order, determine the means and methods by which government agencies conduct business.

The president must also decide whether or not to sign bills passed by Congress into law. That decision will nearly always involve a few compromises. It is up to the President to vouch for the process by which Congress passes bills to provide a failsafe for the public against abuses of power by Congress even when that abuse comes from within the party from which he/she was elected. In other words, the President must have a form of independence from the legislative branch of the government in order to perfect his/her duties in terms of the balance of power the Constitution implies. Likewise, Congress has the power to override the will of the President if the President vetoes legislation that is supported by more than two/thirds of both houses of Congress.

The President is also vested with the authority, as discussed earlier, to conduct foreign policy. This role, more than any other, forces the President to consider what is best for the nation above the interests of his/her party. It was significant, for example, that England's former Prime Minister, Tony Blair, considered first the interest of his country in supporting the military actions in both Afghanistan and Iraq. Mr. Blair's ruling Labour Party, like the Democrat Party in America, did not, for the most part support the action in Iraq in particular – especially after the war had begun. In spite of his own party's opposition, Mr. Blair consistently supported the action in alliance with the United States recognizing that conditions often require an Executive Leader in any government to support issues where the nation's best interest in the long term conflict with its short term agenda.

Imagine, if you will, a different sort of experience that could happen if a future American President saw the wisdom of George Washington in appropriately separating the powers of the Presidency from the interests of the political party with whom he/she was elected. What would happen if on the eve of the State of the Union Address, the President's speech (let's assume for purposes here that he was a Democrat) went something like this:

"Good evening. My highly esteemed colleagues, members of the House, Senate, members of our nation's Supreme Court and my fellow Americans, I stand before you tonight in this, the People's House to fulfill my duty in presenting the State of our Union.

As I stand here tonight I am cognizant of the fact that our nation has experienced a widening separation in opinion between the two major parties that have traditionally supplied our nation's leaders in Congress and the office within which I am now privileged to serve. During our nation's history the rise and fall of competing ideologies followed a gentle course that responded for the most part to the major crises of each succeeding generation. Throughout our nation's development it has often been the case that our government responded to the people's urgent desires only after those desires reached a stage of critical mass. In some ways our two-party system has delayed the nation's response as two sometimes vastly different ideologies struggled to address a crisis. We cannot escape the reality that here, in America, the ideological divide slows down our response time but often creates a more moderate approach that, in the end, generally serves the nation well.

That is why I am particularly honored tonight to address members of this Congress who, from both sides of the isle, have given this nation their heart and soul along with the hours, days, months and years of their own lives. In addressing you that are seated here tonight I am keenly aware that what you will hear tonight from me might be shocking but it is not without precedent. Our nation's first President did not enjoy the privilege of being elected by the people. He did have the honor of being elected by members of Congress who fought with him in gaining our nation's independence. He, more than anyone else, seemed to possess the humility to recognize that our nation would never survive if the Presidency became something too near the monarchy from which we gained our liberty. George Washington knew there had to be a unique and strong bond of trust between the American people and their President.

Our first President was wise enough to question the role political parties might play in diverting a future President's attention from the responsibility to carry out his duties to all the people. As our nation has matured so has our ability to communicate. With the advent of internet technology our citizens can know what you and I are doing (and sometimes just thinking of doing) before members of our own staffs. The recent crises we face seem to have found a pace consistent with the speed of that communication. In fact, if you watch the news tonight you'll no doubt hear what I said, didn't say and should have said. In fact, my speech here tonight might just be tomorrow's first crisis. That is why, frankly, I didn't allow the transcript of this speech to be advanced to the media and why all of you here tonight do not have a copy either. I guess you'll all have to figure out on your own when to stand and when to applaud.

I do want to say that tonight of all nights I owe a great debt of gratitude to the Democrat party from which I gained support and with whom I have fought to bring my party's solutions into the arena of the possible. From the caucuses in Iowa to the general election in November I have rarely missed a meal (that's one reason this suit is new and improved with a spandex waist band) nor did I fail to hear your words of encouragement. You have carried me on the wave of your enthusiasm and proved, once again, that becoming the President of the United States is the greatest honor that anyone could ever receive. It is also the reason that I have chosen to take this responsibility in the spirit of our first President.

Tonight, I am declaring my own independence from the Democrat party that I love and will always love. I am not doing so because I have had a change of heart. I am doing so because I have a heart for the Office and history that demands more from a President than mere party fidelity. I realize that the election results were close. I would not have the privilege of serving as President without at least some Republicans (disoriented as they may have been) voting for me and for the policies I promised to pursue. In saying this I am also aware that my opponent from November's election deservedly holds the respect, honor and loyalty of the many Americans whose vote declared a friendly (well, usually friendly) opposition to my stated policies and platform. So, before I continue I want to acknowledge my opponent, his undying patriotism, his fidelity to the principles of his party and my deepest confidence that he will remain a member of the loyal opposition during my administration. Governor Landau, I salute you and I trust all of America honors you for the clear commitment you made in offering your services to this nation. I hope that I will never again have to look over my shoulder to see if you are there. Instead I hope to see you by my side when those things on which we agree are implemented with the help of this Congress.

In declaring my independence from the Democrat Party I am also declaring my independence from any party. I believe the office of the President requires this independence so that, as the leader of the executive branch of our government I may have the option of listening to the opposition and negotiating with them in good faith to win them over when I can and to win with them when they have succeeded in convincing the people of this country that theirs is the better vision for a particular issue. This is the job of the

President and why, ultimately, the buck stopped with Harry Truman and will stop with me as well.

According to the Constitution of this nation, the Vice President is vested with the duty of presiding over the Senate. While this has been a largely ceremonial duty and has only been significant in breaking tie votes within that body, I am asking that Vice President Larson accept this important role along with that of leading and directing the Democrat Party in my stead. I will ask that he do all that is in his power to forward and advance the Democrat agenda including representing that view to me in the Oval Office and to all Americans as well. As of tonight I will no longer communicate with the DNC, or other organs of the Democrat Party as an "insider." Of course I will regularly meet with the Senate and House leadership and I will give my level best to fulfill every campaign promise made.

One of the reasons I have decided to pursue this course of action is that I am not keen on the idea of spending half of my term in office campaigning for the next. In his role as Vice President I expect Mr. Larson to lead the Democrats in the Senate, lobby Republicans who can't seem to see the world correctly, and to always be ready to take my place should my life end or disability overtake me during my term. I have every reason to believe that my Vice President will prove his worth to this nation and will gain the wisdom that comes with responsible leadership. What he will do will be more valuable to this country than traveling to non-descript locations with gifts from my office for foreign dignitaries.

I am also announcing tonight that I will not actively seek the Democrat nomination for a new term at the end of this term but if I have earned their respect and they choose to re-nominate me I will, by God's grace be ready for the campaign. By not seeking this office I intend to remain a relevant President throughout the entirety of my term in office.

Before I address the specific issues that face our nation I want to take a moment to illustrate my resolve to independently consider all solutions to our nation's problems. In order to do so, I would like to direct your attention to the seats where my wife is now sitting. You will immediately recognize my daughters and my wife, Julie. You may not recognize that person sitting behind her but that's okay because I am going to break another tradition by NOT talking about them. I would like, instead, for the distinguished Senator from Wisconsin, Mr. Abernathy, to stand.

Senator, I want to address you this evening because you have faithfully served the Republican Party in times where you were in the minority as well as times when you led the Republican charge as Majority Leader. In your service you have been reelected four times and will be moving into your 23rd year in service to our nation. You have always been loyal to this nation and I want all of America to know that. While I truly hate to face you in debate and I rarely like your ideas, I do not hate you.

We share a love for this country that binds us together regardless of our differing principles. Our principles may be different but I will never accuse you of being without principles. I want your State to know that they have done a good thing in sending you here. Your voice, though too often an irritant to me, is a voice that I must, nevertheless hear and try to understand. You will always find that my door is open to you. I must confess that I hope your State will one day see the light and send someone else here but I have to also confess that I truly hope whoever is sent here from Wisconsin will have at least half of the character and integrity you possess.

I could stand here tonight and give honor to a few others for whom I have developed a true loving respect and that would naturally include some of my close friends on the left of this beautiful House. The point is this, your President has to be the President of all Americans and that means sometimes having to acknowledge the will of the people and act accordingly. It means honestly appreciating the tasks of a loyal opposition party and the loyal opponents within it. I will not be afraid to choose a contrarian path even when a majority of Americans disagree with me. Sometimes I will have to act on the principles I have clearly stated in the campaign and hope that history will ultimately support the choices for which I alone am accountable. In any case, we all know that this nation will have to decide in another four years whether or not my return to the tradition of George Washington was wise or foolish.

So, let's move forward with the way our nation should prosecute the war on terror..."

Whether this speech was given by a Democrat or Republican is irrelevant to the point. The question is whether any President would have the courage of conviction to fulfill the responsibility of the Presidency in the spirit in which that Office was created by our Constitution. The Constitution's separation of powers has become dysfunctional because of party politics. The President cannot uphold his/her Constitutional duty to faithfully execute the duties of President if party politics continues to create political obligations that trump the will of the people and the moral imperative to simply do the right thing.

Separation of Powers – *Congress*

House of Representatives

The House of Representatives is the body which most closely represents individual Americans. Members are elected from districts that are established by each individual State and are subject to boundaries created by State Legislatures. It is therefore entirely possible that members of a national majority may find themselves in the minority within the districts in which they happen to reside.

Even so, Christian theology mandates the acceptance of those conditions once an election has taken place. In other words Christian Americans should accept as fact that the individual sovereignty held by all voters in a district is expressed through the ballot box and an elected Representative can act on behalf of all voters in the election – even those who voted against him/her.

Our Representatives are also responsible to uphold and faithfully defend the Constitution. That document, among other things, embodies the concept of the separation of powers and the duly elected Representative's responsibility to protect the natural rights of his/her constituents and constituent families. Christians, then, must hold their

Representatives accountable through direct and indirect correspondence. The level to which a Christian must be active cannot be understated. More than anything else the duty to vote must be supplemented by the duty to be active and vigilant.

Members of the House must face an election every two years but the power of incumbency has been historically significant. Once a Representative takes office in the House, the advantages of that office are significant in terms of communicating with constituents using free postage and the power to affect a consistent image using all present forms of the media.

There has been much more discussion in the past two decades about term limits which can be set by state legislatures. These efforts, for the most part, have failed because it is in a state's best interest to have Representatives gain seniority in the House where that seniority opens access to powerful committees and potential chairmanships of those committees.

The system of seniority in the House is derived from the rules of the House. These rules (about 53 pages of single-spaced legalese) concentrate power in the majority party and specifically in the power of that party's internally elected leadership. Christians must understand the role of the Speaker of The House and the majority party leadership when it comes to advancing economic and political policy. It is a difficult process to understand but a simple and straight-forward explanation here might help draw an understandable picture of how things really work in the House.

The Constitution simply states that the House itself chooses its Speaker. This accommodation was primarily to preserve order and decorum for a body (now 435 members) that could become unruly in debate. In subsequent sections of Article 1 of the Constitution, Congress was granted the prerogative to construct rules of conduct in each house respectively. These rules would be the instrument through which officers of the House, committees, and committee chairman would be selected.

The rules for the House of Representatives are ratified at the beginning of each Congress and generally contain most of the previous Congress' rules and any changes that might be applied by a new incoming majority. The rules are then approved on an "up or down" vote.

The broad range of power inherent in the majority party's position is evidenced by that party's ability to determine which committees in Congress are "Standing" or permanent committees. Likewise it provides for the creation of a limitless number of non-permanent committees to handle the legislative work and oversight of the House. Within these committees the Speaker of the House, the Majority Leader and the Minority Leader establish who among their respective party membership will serve on each committee.

The seniority system that has evolved over the history of both the House and the Senate has created a situation that, for American Christians, contradicts the principles of individual sovereignty upon which our founding fathers constructed the Constitution. This is admittedly open for debate among Christians and non-Christians alike but the result of the seniority system is plainly evident. American citizens who send a <u>new</u> Representative to the House are systemically underrepresented by that member when compared to members of Congress who have been reelected several times.

The short duration of the Representative's term (two years) and the fact that the House of Representatives was envisioned as the "People's House" clearly show that the founding fathers preferred that it be filled with citizen-legislators who would not make a career of being a Representative. On the contrary it was envisioned that ordinary citizens would have the opportunity to participate in Government as a deterrent to a permanent "ruling class."

The power to limit a Representative's years in office, however, was vested in the right of citizens to vote not in an arbitrary limitation of terms within the Constitution. This assured that citizens would remain active in politics and always abreast of local, state and world events. The seniority system, however, has thwarted the intent of the Constitution's framers making it difficult for citizens from a congressional district to have an immediate impact on issues that are important to them but perhaps not as important to a district somewhere else in the country.

The powers that the majority party in the House enjoys are not the problem. Power, in a democratic republic, is intended to be significant for the majority. It is the execution of those powers in limiting the impact of new Representatives by virtue of their simply being "new" to the body. The seniority system forces an underrepresentation for districts whose citizens have rights equal to those of any other district in the nation.

Given this circumstance American Christians must seek to retain the authority of our God-endowed natural rights by becoming and remaining more active in the political process and by doing everything within our power to eliminate the seniority system in both the House and the Senate. They should seek to ensure that it is this aspect of Christian theology that motivates the economic and political policy of the candidates they support and then work hard to get them elected.

American Christians need to understand the power of a personal connection to their Representative. Regular phone calls and e-mails to their office will help to establish a recognizable pattern and your "bona fides" as his/her staff assesses the daily call log and the persuasiveness of your position.

In addition, a personal visit to the Congressman's local office during a recess of the House should be considered an <u>annual imperative</u>. It is virtually impossible for a Representative to the Congress to personally know even a small fraction of his/her constituents. This is why it is well worth the investment to include a trip to Washington, D.C. at least once during a Representative's tenure in the House. Every American Christian should make it a goal to have at least one family member make this trip every four years. Visiting your Representative and both Senators from your State isn't a privilege, it's a right.

Making the most of your visit and maximizing the impact of the opinions you wish to register requires advance planning and the ability to remain respectful at all times. Whether you are attending a town hall meeting, visiting with your Representative at his/her local office or making the trip to the Nation's Capital, Christian theology dictates that your demeanor and comportment always remain consistent with the character of Christ.

Always make a formal appointment, weeks in advance, if you want to personally visit your Representative or Senator. Keep your questions brief and to the point. Don't load your question or statements with presuppositions that force your Representative to hedge or equivocate on an answer. Be respectful by expressing genuine gratitude for a Representative's service to America (even if you believe his/her actions are mostly a disservice to your agenda).

Start your discussion (realizing that you may have less than a few minutes of his/her time) with a clear statement of your own agenda. Don't argue your agenda; just state your belief in simple terms understanding that your objective is to force the Representative to either support your agenda or at least express the rational support for his/her competing idea. It is better if you come away from a personal meeting having heard what he/she said to you than saying what you think the Representative needed to hear.

Why is that the case? Because once you understand the fundamental basis of a Representative's opinion you can make your follow up communications (by phone or by mail) more pertinent and effective. At some point in time you may come to the realization that your Representative simply does not share your fundamental faith in the Sovereignty of God but instead has placed his/her faith in humanity and the competing theology of humanism. If this is true you will be able to cogently and convincingly describe that to your friends and fellow believers who also vote.

If you have succeeded in getting a Representative's attention you may find that he/she will direct you to a legislative aide. Do not be offended. This is a good thing. In fact you will note that Representatives often have a legislative aide in his/her local office. These are people that you should routinely visit. Get to know what they are working on and ask them to help you understand how to get specific ideas incorporated into current or future legislation.

When you attend a town hall meeting held by your Representative you will quickly notice that some in attendance like to hear their own voice. You will witness arrogance and anger. Neither of these should be tools in a Christian's tool bag. It is not appropriate to use invectives or spiteful ad hominem attacks (these are attacks on the person rather than on the policy or belief system).

You may very well think that your Representative is an idiot but it is never appropriate to express or imply that thought in a civil discourse. Smile when you ask a question. Smile when you state a fact and always thank the Representative for making the forum possible. Remember as well that all of the meeting's attendees are listening to and watching you as well. If you are successful they may not necessarily remember you but they will understand and remember point you made. Document everything you do, say or write when communicating with your Representative. However, remember that video-taping or running a digital phone's video should never be done without the Representative's knowledge and approval. This is not a "legal" requirement; it is a righteous requirement.

When you find a Representative that has earned your trust and confirmed their adherence to Christian theology, you should get out your check book, right there right then, and contribute to that Representative's campaign. As the election nears you should also volunteer to make phone calls, knock on doors and post yard signs in your yard as well as those of your friends who share your belief and give their consent.

There may be times (more often in fact that any of us would like) that your Representative agrees with a majority of your beliefs but significantly departs from a few of your firmly held convictions. Rather than fall into despair and anger, volunteer your services to advance those policies on which you agree. There is no reason that an American Christian can't support a Representative from either major party when that Representative is willing to push even one issue that is critical to defending our natural rights. Christians in America desperately need to disassociate themselves with party politics and, instead, associate themselves with the definable economic and political policies supported by solid Christian theology.

Separation of Powers – *Congress*

The United States Senate

Each State in America sends two Senators to the United States Senate. Senators serve a longer term than Representatives to the House (six years as opposed to two years). This extended term provides Senators with more insulation from the emotional upheavals common to political winds that rapidly change. It is a body intended to be more deliberative and therefore more cautious in considering major changes in America law.

It is the Senate that confirms Supreme Court nominees because they are less subject to reelection considerations that might too heavily influence their vote. In contrast to your Representative in the House, you may find your Senator is not as energized about local issues and may not be particularly motivated by issues that impact your own state, particularly if your state's Governor is in the same political party. Senators tend to develop a "national" paradigm and seriously take the responsibility to assure that the direction of the nation isn't controlled by more populous and more powerful States.

Having to represent the entire State forces Senators to a schedule that seriously hampers their ability to make time for personal visits. In the case of Senators it is far more advantageous for a citizen to contact and work with the Senator's legislative aides.

The advent of the internet has allowed Senators to communicate with their constituents in real time. While the communications might look personal they are anything but that. In fact the process of responding to citizen messages has been computerized to electronically sort your messages, determine its intent through key word searches and to construct a computer generated response from the Senator's collection of "Position Statements."

Position Statements are a collection of the Senator's written and verbal statements addressing a wide range of current legislation or policy agendas. Your calls into the Senator's office are documented and your opinions are sorted and reported to the Senator on a daily basis. American Christians may not have as much access to their Senators but they have three times the amount of time to develop a personal rapport with them or their legislative aides.

Making use of this time requires consistency. If you want to have an impact on a Senator's policy you have to be committed to a program of regular and timely contact. Patience is critical. There is nothing more powerful than lending your hands, feet and voice to those issues on which you and your Senator agree.

This is a good point to share a personal story: As a freshman in college I was able to make a trip to Washington, D.C. for a two-week program. The program was aimed at Christian college students and provided a one-week symposium including some very special speakers. We heard from Chuck Colson (a key Watergate player who was sent to prison for his crimes and converted to Christianity while he was incarcerated). The newly appointed Supreme Court Justice (and later Chief Justice of the Supreme Court), William Rehnquist, met with our group at the Supreme Court and spent a good deal of time answering our questions.

During the second week of our program each student was assigned to either a U.S. Senator or a Representative of the House as an intern. I had the great privilege of being assigned to Senator John (Jack) C. Danforth's office. He was a Republican from the State of Missouri. Senator Danforth had just been elected in the previous November elections of 1975 for the term commencing in January of 1976. I arrived at his office on a Monday morning in early January.

As I came through the door with youthful apprehension I was met with a scene that can only be described as chaos. Secretaries, administrative assistants and various other people were flying around in apparent confusion. The office itself had only been assigned to the Senator days before I arrived. I suddenly turned to hear a yelp coming from behind me. It was Senator Danforth excitedly hurrahing over his new committee assignments. He managed to be placed on two committees critical to his agenda.

A friendly looking woman finally approached me. She was the Senator's press secretary. She smiled broadly and took me back to a small desk where banker's boxes were piled on the top and spilling over on the sides of the desk as well. "These," she said as she pointed at the boxes, "are the Senator's position papers. They are in alphabetical order by subject matter," she continued. She tossed a stack of opened letters in front of me. "Read these," she ordered, "figure out the main topic of the letter and then find the corresponding position paper in one of these boxes."

I was prepared early on that my work for the week would mostly be perfunctory paper pushing, perhaps just opening mail. Her next set of instructions absolutely astonished me.

"Take the corresponding position paper and read it thoroughly." I looked up at her and she was still smiling. "Then I want you to draft a letter of response from the Senator." She pulled a piece of paper off her desk and handed it to me. "These are the introductory paragraphs and closing paragraphs that you can use to begin and end the letter – be careful to address your letters to the constituent personally."

She walked away with a confident stride leaving me feeling like the most important intern to ever walk the hall of the Senate. I went to work with a passion and responded to some twenty or so letters that day. I typed the letters on an electric typewriter and stacked them on the press secretary's desk before leaving for my hotel around 6:00 pm.

That evening the ten or twelve students from my small Christian college went to dinner at a local Chinese restaurant. I was very excited to hear about everyone's day and listened as each student rehearsed their experience for the group. I was particularly excited to hear from one of my truly good friends whose father was a State Senator in Florida. He, my friend, was clearly connected because he had been placed in the office of Senator Lawton Chiles from Florida. He was already personally acquainted with the Senator and so we all assumed he would be getting more than most of us from his internship experience.

As the discussion around the table started, I realized that I would the last to share. Each student consistently stated they had spent the day in the mail room mostly just opening letters and sorting them by issue. One was assigned to a Representative from the State of Washington and spent his morning delivering smoked salmon to various other offices in the Russell Building. The discussion moved on my friend from Florida. Everyone leaned in across their dinner plates to hear. "I worked in to gol-dang mail room." he drawled. His easy-going demeanor made us laugh with him. Even the well-connected had to spend at least a day in the mail room.

Finally it was my turn and I explained what I had done that day and I became the new center of attention. However, nothing could prepare me for the events of the next day.

I entered the office and immediately went to the press secretary's desk where I assumed I would get another stack of letters from which to draft responses. Instead, she took through another doorway inside the office where I was introduced to Senator Danforth's legislative aide. He asked me to take a seat and spent about three minutes explaining what a legislative aide does. He then took the letters I had written the day before and reviewed a few of them with me. Standing, he took the letters over to a bulky machine that had a felt-tipped pen lodged in a circular ring attached to two robotic arms. Pushing a button and placing a letter under the pen I watched as "Senator Danforth 1A-2" signed the letter.

Then he turned around to face his desk and pulled a large manila envelope from the top of the desk. Its contents were burgeoning through a few cuts on the corners of the envelope. As he poured the contents across his desk he picked up the letter that I guessed explained the rest of the contents.

"This," he said, "is a letter from a fairly important constituent outside St. Louis, Missouri. He has been a loyal campaigner for the Senator dating back to the Senator's term as Missouri's Attorney General. I want you read what he writes about a particular piece of watershed legislation that will be taken up in the Senate this year. The watershed area in question crosses his land and so he has requested the Senator's help in protecting his land rights. You are going to have to get a copy of that current statute, read it, and then write a synopsis for me of the pertinent issues in the statute and in this man's letter. After we have discussed it, you will draft a letter of response to the constituent, I'll review it, and then the Senator will sign it."

I asked him where I would be able to find the referenced statute and he picked up the phone. "You have to call over the Library of Congress." He handed me the phone and dialed the number leaving me to talk to someone in the Library of Congress who answered with a rather plaintive hello.

Within a couple of hours I was looking at a copy of the statute and began attempting to prepare a response. Needless to say my internship in Washington would not have been so eventful had I stumbled into Senator Danforth's office two years later when he and his staff would be fully organized. For me, timing was everything. In the chaos of just opening the doors of a new Senator's office I was able to do a lot and learn a lot.

As an intern, working as a volunteer, I was able to make friendships and connections that would otherwise have been impossible. Interestingly enough my contacts with the Senator's staff meant more to my future than anything I gained from the very brief personal visit I had with the Senator on the third day of my internship. In that meeting he was very kind and courteous. He is a tall man with a booming voice that seemed like an echo of his previous occupation as an Episcopalian Pastor.

I was only able to talk with him while we stood for a photograph that he would give me on the day I left for home. I mentioned to him that it seemed odd to me that someone could be a Christian minister and a politician. The Senator looked down at me for a moment and said, "Oh, I don't think the two occupations are that different at all... I think our country needs more Christian influence not less."

Separation of Powers – *The Judiciary*

The Supreme Court

I remember the day that I came home from work and tuned into a national news broadcast. Senator Danforth's voice once again captured my attention. He was sitting at a bank of desks placed before the Senate's Judiciary Committee. At his side sat Clarence Thomas. Senator Danforth had developed a close friendship with the future Justice over the years – Thomas had been an Assistant Attorney General in Missouri in 1974 and became Senator Danforth's legislative assistant in 1979.

Years later, after his nomination and appointment to the Supreme Court, Thomas wrote an autobiography and I found myself listening to the book on tape as I drove to a sales meeting. In one chapter Thomas discussed his time in Danforth's office and mentioned the very people I had met there as well. I smiled to myself as I remembered the impact that single week – working in Danforth's office – had on my own life. Although I never met Clarence Thomas I felt a unique kinship listening to his voice as his described Danforth's.

The Constitution of the United States vests the responsibility for holding Congress and the

President accountable to the rule of law in the Judiciary and specifically, the Supreme Court. With nine Justices, the Court meets on the first Monday in October each year to begin a new session. The Court reviews cases that have been submitted from the Nation's Circuit Courts and those cases where the Court has expressed interest because of time sensitivity.

With respect to the separation of powers and the Christian theological principle of sovereignty, the Court must itself be held accountable to retain the original intentions of our Nation's founding fathers when the Constitution was written. At this time there are only two avenues for holding the Court accountable and that is for Congress to either pass a law that circumvents the "unconstitutional" elements of a previously passed law or to amend the Constitution itself (a process that will require ¾ of all States to ratify the amendment. Individual Justices are held accountable only through the difficult process of impeachment.

The problem for American Christians is that the Court has often reached beyond the scope of the Constitution to invent "rights" that cannot be read from the document but must be read "into" the document.

Over the past three decades the process of confirming Supreme Court Justices has become nothing less than comic drama. In an effort to pack the court with Justices that are sympathetic to the sitting President's interpretive agenda, nominees are routinely selected from a list of candidates that matches the President's political leanings. In addition it has become routine for a President to attempt to match a nominee to the outgoing or deceased Justice's race or gender. Justices rarely retire until a President of their own party is able to replace them. But in the event that a Justice dies in office the President will generally work hard to swing the Court in either the liberal or conservative bias he/she prefers.

For its part, the Senate has crumbled under its constitutional duty to properly screen nominees for the Supreme Court. Nominees have resorted to refusing to answer questions that might tip Senators off to their interpretation of the Constitution's various articles.

By virtue of having been nominated by a sitting President it should be no great secret that the nominee is at least sympathetic to the agenda of the President's political party. However, the task of adjudicating our nation's laws and their constitutionality requires more than holding one's finger in the air to discern the political winds of the present. A Supreme Court Justice's appointment is a life appointment. It is therefore absolutely necessary for the Senate to know exactly how a nominee will interpret critical elements of the Constitution and whether or not they consider the document the final arbiter of America's laws. It has become clear that some of the current sitting Justices (and perhaps the most recently confirmed Justice, Elena Kagan) feel free to defer to foreign laws when deciding to uphold or strike down portions of American legislation.

 For American Christians this is unacceptable. Nominees to the Supreme Court must be forced to answer reasonable questions where the answer articulates the nominee's interpretation of any or all parts of the Constitution. Senators in the minority party are routinely stonewalled when they present reasonable questions that are admittedly aimed to uncover a nominee's political agenda.

The framers of our Constitution did not seek to disqualify potential justices because of their political views. Neither did the framers intend to insulate nominees from exposing what those political views were. Senators, in exercising their duties to the electorate, have every right to determine whether or not a nominee will be either an originalist or an activist when determining the Constitutionality of any legislation or judgment of a lower Court.

Nominees have recently refused to answer some questions for fear that they will then be obliged to recuse themselves from hearing cases where the question they answer might indicate a prejudicial view that circumvents the impartiality of the Court. The idea that a nominee cannot convey a principle of interpretation without voiding their impartiality in a particular case is intellectually vacuous.

After the Health Care Reform Act of 2010 was signed into law the current nominee to the Court, Elena Kagan, was asked by Senator Tom Coburn, (R) Oklahoma, whether the Constitution's Commerce Clause could allow the federal government to pass a law requiring citizens to eat three vegetable a day. Kagan obfuscated by claiming that such a law would be a "stupid" law. She went on to opine that the Supreme Court couldn't throw a law out just because it happened to be "stupid." In answering this way she did not address the actual point of the Senator's question.

The point of Coburn's question was that the Commerce Clause might be grounds for striking down the Health Care Reform Act's requirement that all Americans buy health insurance. Several state Attorneys General have already filed suit against the law claiming that it is a violation of the Commerce Clause – that the federal government cannot force individuals to buy a product or service.

While it is true that Coburn's question was only thinly veiled it was nonetheless completely appropriate and should have been truthfully answered. When Kagan stated that a law requiring citizens to eat three vegetables a day was stupid, Coburn retorted that he "knew another law that was equally stupid." A Supreme Court Justice's duty is to interpret the Constitution, not make law. Had Kagan honestly answered the Senator's question she would have revealed her interpretation of the Clause's impact on whether the government can force citizens to eat three vegetable a day but she would not have thereby eliminated her ability to evaluate the constitutionality of the Health Care and Reform Act of 2010. Notice the word, "ability." Having answered the question honestly, the Senate would certainly have a clue as to how the nominee would vote on a similarly framed law but answering the question would have no impact on Kagan's future abilities.

The Senate should be pressured by American Christians to force nominees to either answer legitimate questions or remove themselves from consideration for America's highest court. Without this power the Senate cannot enforce the separation of powers outlined in the Constitution.

What It Means to Be Created Equal

"We hold these truths to be self-evident, that all men are created equal..." So says the Declaration of Independence. It's one reason many Americans believe that those living in America should be treated equally.

Americans will nearly unanimously argue the essential civil rights outlined in the Bill of Rights and amendments to the Constitution are part of the American birthright. These rights have been progressively established in law so that no one should be discriminated against on the basis of race, religion, gender or, in some States, sexual orientation.

The extent to which humans are created equal, however, rarely receives genuine intellectual attention. The Declaration of Independence *partially* defines our equality by reference, citing our right to life, liberty and the pursuit of happiness. The definition of each of these rights has traditionally been left to the Judiciary branch of our government to interpret. But Congress has also weighed in to either expand or limit these rights in response to our dynamic history.

Throughout the historic changes in the definition of what is a right (or an entitlement) of citizenship, the nation has rarely been treated to a discussion of what being created "equal" actually means.

This failure has resulted in the frequent use of the word "equality" in discussions without acknowledging that its meaning varies among individual citizens. The result is that we are all talking <u>at</u> each other but certainly not communicating <u>with</u> one another when we speak of equality.

Simple observation reveals that not all humans are really created equal when it comes to physical or mental capacity. We are not automatons stamped out at a heavenly factory. We look different and act different in ways that make the human race incalculably diverse. Human personality and behavioral traits emerge within months of birth. One need only visit a primary school classroom to see that by the age of 4 or 5 years, humans begin to separate themselves by differences in performance.

One clear example of this form of "inequality" can be witnessed each year when any professional sport league holds its annual draft of amateur athletes. It is true that an occasional late round draftee surprises everyone and performs as well as a first round draft choice. But the system is built around the assumption that a first round draftee will outperform those drafted in later rounds. They will also collect much larger signing bonuses.

Because of their unique talents (but particularly because their talents entertain us) athletes, actors, authors and artists of different stripes rarely have to justify their incomes to average Americans. Some talented and well-paid individuals among us are routinely accused of things like greed and overindulgence, however, simply because their particular talents aren't "entertaining."

Wall Street brokers, for example, seldom get endorsement deals from Nike. Famous athletes or actors who fail to keep on entertaining us eventually see the curtain of criticism fall on them as well. Suddenly they begin to face the "compensation jury" of average, normal Americans. As long as they do entertain us, they are adopted like our own children as though they represent our national DNA. But those who achieve wealth by taking risks without really entertaining anyone are simply considered "lucky" or "fortunate."

A growing number of Americans seem to believe that very high incomes are a sign that our nation has lost sight of a basic belief in the equality of all human beings. To them, it seems unethical that someone who just happens to be more talented should be paid such outlandish salaries. It appears unfair that only a few can win the DNA lottery in life.

It is understandable that many of us experience simple jealousy from time to time. It is altogether something different, however, to feel justified in staking a claim on someone else's productivity because we feel their "luck" is our "misfortune."

The argument for seizing a portion of that "lucky fortune" and redistributing it to those who are "less fortunate" is that the American economic system is what makes it possible for the "fortunate" to amass their "fortune." It is often stated that these successful Americans could not have been successful without the culture of liberty and capitalism our nation provides.

American Christians understand this is true. They "get it."

Our national charter (the Constitution), our national soul (the Declaration of Independence) and our national spirit (the sacrificial performance of our military forces) have made our nation a place where excellence leads to the opportunity to accumulate personal wealth.

Extraordinary achievements of the fortunate are not *always* criticized. After all, most Americans have at least one or two overachievers in their own family. But America's fixation with equality has progressively evolved to the point where being created "equal" has come to mean that we are all "entitled" to share in each other's income. It's one thing for your mom or dad to approach Uncle Kevin to ask that he help you find a position in his successful company. Even in families, however, it is not a given that Uncle Kevin will show up at the annual family picnic with checks for everyone in the family. And yet, this is just what has become of the American system of income taxation.

Christians have to work hard to help the nation redefine two terms: greed and compassion. They are two sides of the same coin. From the perspective of keeping what is ours or staking a claim on someone else's income the word "greed" applies. But from the viewpoint that God really has created everyone with the same natural rights but not the same talents the word "compassion" has to enter the conversation.

There is a story in the New Testament about the Apostles Peter and John. Shortly after the death and resurrection of Jesus, they were on their way into the Temple to promote the faith they had placed in Jesus. A lame man at the entrance to the Temple reached his hand out to beg for money. Peter, overwhelmed with compassion but poor himself, looked down on the man on the ground.

Something came over Peter as he seemed to realize just what this man really needed and it wasn't a handout. Taking the man by the hand Peter said to him, "I don't have any silver or gold either. But what I do have I will give to you." Lifting the man up from the ground Peter said, "In the name of Jesus, stand up and walk!"

Can you imagine what people around this scene were thinking? They no doubt thought Peter was insane, mean or vicious. To their amazement, and no doubt John's, strength entered into the lame man's legs and he began to walk and leap around in sheer joy.

From a theological standpoint there are four messages in this event. The first is that Christians must be compassionate about the fact that not everyone is created equal when it comes to life's DNA lottery. The second is that God, in his Sovereign role as both the Creator and Sustainer of our existence is ready, willing and able to heal anyone and meet the real needs in their life. Our nation needs to return to this fundamental understanding and belief. The third message is that God expects us, like Peter and John, to be the ones lending a hand up when God decides to bring healing and comfort into the lives of others. The final message is really plain. Silver and gold alone aren't enough to meet the needs of the poor or infirmed in our society.

Lending a hand up to others is our duty and responsibility in this world. The question is not whether we should be willing to do that. The question is how best to lend a hand. Peter was confronted by some leaders of the Jewish faith shortly after this took place and he was very quick to tell them that what happened had nothing to do with his own power. He told them in clear terms that he was a human just like anyone else. He emphatically stated that it was God who really performed the miracle.

In the same way Christians in America have to willing to extend compassion to others understanding that it is God's work to actually lift people up from their physical, emotional or spiritual handicaps.

The problem with America's current income tax code is that compassion is eliminated from the process because the tax is compulsory and not voluntary. It is not compassionate to comply with a law where no personal choice is involved. We are compelled to pay our income taxes or suffer the legal penalties. The compulsory income tax also removes God from the event. Instead of cooperating with his awesome power to produce miracles in the everyday lives of our citizens the government has supplanted God by trying to be the vehicle through which people's needs are met.

Statistics about taxation are readily available on the internet and are frequently used by conservatives to illustrate how the real tax burden in this country is borne by those who earn the most. Although you may have seen these figures before and heard the same old lines, take a fresh look at them. Try to think in terms of whether the current tax code elicits greed or illustrates national compassion.

According to The Tax Foundation, and using IRS data reported for 2008, these points might help you decide:

1. In 2008, the top 1% of income earners (those making $410,096 and higher) paid 40.4% of all federal income taxes.
2. In the same year, the bottom 95% (those making zero to $160,041) paid 39.4% of all federal income taxes.

3. The bottom 50% of all income earners (those making less than $32,879) paid just 2.9% of all federal income taxes.
4. 36.3% of all Americans who filed an income tax return paid no federal income tax at all.

All human beings are created with equal rights yet it is just as evident that Americans aren't treated equally when it comes to paying income taxes. The top 1% of our nation now pays more than the entire bottom 95% combined. That's not all, it was possible in 2008 for a family of four to make as much as $55,583 and have their tax obligation entirely offset by the combination of stimulus checks of $1,200 per couple plus $300 per child.

Some of the 36.3% of Americans who paid no federal income tax could have made as much as $55,000.

It is little wonder that our nation now has a movement afoot calling itself, the "Tea Party." Are all of these people in the top 5% of the nation's income earners? Is that why they are taking it to the streets? That's not likely because according to various polls, between 18 and 24% of all American voters identify themselves with one of the several tea party organizations.

They can't all be paying exorbitant taxes. Are they just angry and embittered right wing fanatics? No doubt some are but recent polls of the group show that they are much more diverse, in terms of political parties, gender, age, etc. than initially reported by the media. Perhaps what is really driving the Tea Party is that our current government is moving down a path of social spending (based on an ideal that all Americans should benefit equally from our productivity) that is unsustainable. What would happen if those in the top 5% of income earners decided to leave the country? High income earners are already vacating New Jersey and New York because those States continue to raise taxes on the wealthy to fund the needs of the growing poverty class. They know they can conduct their businesses elsewhere in the nation.

The amount of our current federal deficits each year and the mounting national debt will require more and more confiscation of America's individual income. Taxing only 1% of our nation's earners will not be enough. Soon, everyone will be paying much higher taxes, including those who can ill afford to do so.

The question that must be answered is simple:

Are we really created equal and, if so, does that mean that American Christians should agree to share everything with everyone?

To honestly answer that question we have to take a closer look at just one word in the question: "created".

That word presupposes first, a Creator. If Americans are, as the Declaration expresses, "created" who is that Creator? Americans are certainly not in agreement on whether that is even true in the first place and yet we all seem bent on claiming the benefits of the equality that Creator is supposed to have granted. Those who choose to believe in a Creator (and it is a choice) must answer the question of whether or not that Creator has anything to say about the "self-evident" truth of our equality.

In the Bible, God says some amazing things about our individual equality. He declares that he is not partial toward one human being over another – each individual is equally cherished. Yet it is possible for a person (like Noah for example) to be singled out for a critical mission that includes an incredible blessing.

The rain of the great flood fell on all of humanity but only Noah and his family were within the protection of the ark. That particular event was a form of global punishment for all of humanity's failure to acknowledge God as their Creator.

There is a portion of Scripture that simply states that the rain falls on both the good and the bad. Rains, during the Great Flood, weren't considered a blessing by anyone but the rain mentioned here is a metaphor. It means that the sustaining power of rainfall is for all of humanity whether they believe there is a Creator or not. Regardless of whether or not an individual human acknowledges God as the Creator, that person is just as likely to benefit from the resources God has granted all of humans. This clearly means that God created humanity with equality of "value" to himself. That value isn't something humans earn. It doesn't come to us because of what we do or have done. It comes to us as a result of what we are. All of us are his creation.

The word, "created," then, also means that humans are "creatures." If we desire to secure our natural rights or retain the liberties expressed in the Declaration, we must accept the premise that we did not simply create ourselves. It means that someone out there is larger than us and that our "equality" is best expressed not in what we do but to whom we belong.

First, we are individuals. We are unique from one another and yet share equal standing before our common Creator. Each individual has a right to their own pursuit of life, liberty and happiness. Conversely, we do not have the right to claim a share in the pursuits of other individuals. Nevertheless, as Christians, we should extend an invitation to others to share in the rewards of our own pursuits.

When asked what the greatest law (among the laws of the Hebrews) was, Jesus said, "to love the Lord your God with all your heart, soul and mind." He went on to add the second, "and to love your neighbor as yourself." These two laws, Jesus said, summed up the entirety of the Hebrew Law. Jesus even described what a neighbor is when he went on to tell the familiar parable of the "good Samaritan." Humanity's neighbor is humanity, regardless of color or creed.

This is the underlying "theology" that explains the extent to which humanity is created equal and what that equality entails in terms of an individual's pursuit of life, liberty and happiness. Here are some theological conclusions for Christians to consider:

1. No single individual has more equality than any other individual when it comes to our

shared right to pursue life, liberty and happiness. Results will vary because this equality does not even address the variations of skills, talents and capacities of individuals. This equality is based on not what we do but who we are...we are ALL God's creation.

2. It is not only possible but probable that some individuals will produce more than others regardless of whether those individuals believe in a Creator-God or not. This equality rests in nothing more than what an individual DOES with the resources provided in creation for all of humanity.

3. It is also possible to experience the favor of God based not on who we are (his creation) but what we do with what he, by his Sovereignty, has chosen to give us, as individuals, in terms of skills and aptitudes.

4. Experiencing that favor with God has two requirements: We must "love" Him with all of our heart, soul and mind; we must also love our neighbors as much as we love ourselves. This could very well mean sharing our wealth with others but it also means that whatever we do it must be done voluntarily as if we were doing it for ourselves. This is not to suggest that Americans shouldn't use the vehicle of federal taxation to share the burden of

taking care of our neighbor but it does suggest that taxation should never cross the line where giving becomes involuntary and therefore confiscatory.

5. Jesus said that it is better to give than to receive. This kind of behavior may not be instinctive, but the intellectual truth of it is somehow part of our shared experience within creation as creatures. Humans in society with one another have an intellectual predisposition to understand that chronic or enduring dependency leads to despair.

6. Christian theology therefore assumes there is a price to be paid for the protection of citizenship in a society. That price must be paid, at least in part, by ALL citizens. Even with taxes, it is better to give than to receive as long as the giving isn't compulsory but voluntary.

When is it that giving becomes involuntary and therefore confiscatory? That is a good question for both major political parties to consider. Nothing is as sure as death and taxes, right? Can a tax system ever be considered giving? Bill Clinton sure hoped it could when he first began using the term "investment" when referring to tax increases he felt were necessary to balance the federal budget.

Let's be honest, though; no one likes to pay taxes but paying them is necessary for our federal government to provide those services that have been fairly passed by our representative government over the past 97 years since the federal income tax was first enacted.

Therein lays the problem of voluntary versus confiscatory taxation. The income tax system is inherently confiscatory because the tax is calculated on income. It is based on the production of the individual rather than on the individual's voluntary act of purchasing something for their own consumption. An income tax, to be reasonably fair to the desperately poor, must be progressive (charging a higher percentage on those who earn the most) so that those who earn little or even modest incomes aren't driven into deeper despair by income taxes that confiscate money they need to simply survive. If, for example, a person earning $10,000 a year pays 10% in taxes it is much more painful than someone paying 10% on $50,000 earned per year. One would have only $9,000 to live on while and the other has a much easier path with $45,000 left over from taxes to spend as they see fit. In terms of pain...the picture is pretty clear. But when Americans are taxed on production, the very thing we all want (more production) is being penalized.

Instead, Americans should consider a tax on consumption where taxes are paid on everything that is purchased or consumed except those things which are essential to exist. In this way Americans are truly volunteering their tax dollars because they can make that decision each and every time they decide to purchase something. In order for a consumption tax to be gracious to those in society who do not have the capacity to pay a consumption tax AND pay for their basic and essential needs the consumption tax doesn't have to apply to items, like food, clothing, transportation and even shelter.

Converting to a consumption tax, in the place of a federal income tax, would be a very smart thing to do considering the differences in individual production – our inherent "inequality" – while also acknowledging the "equality" we all share in who we are as opposed to what we do. Funds raised through a consumption tax could continue to be spent by Congress on programs that gain a majority vote, including those social programs that we have now and others that may follow.

A consumption tax would also eliminate the need for an internal revenue service since revenue is no longer counted when taxes are paid. This form of taxation is has often been described and discussed under the name, "Fair Tax." Its supporters are growing. One of its chief proponents is the radio talk-show host, Neal Bortz. Information about this plan is also available at www.fairtax.org.

Roe v. Wade: Unintended Consequences

Very few topics unite Christians more than the issue of abortion. It is an issue that deeply affects the relationship between humanity and the Creator to which our Declaration of Independence makes reference. The idea to legally establish a woman's right to choose whether or not to carry a pregnancy to full term emerged in American society rather gradually.

As the nation experienced rapid growth in population and geography it also expanded its cultural diversity in terms of introducing competing views of theology and morality. Beginning with the industrial revolution and the rapid globalization of the economy, America's moral center moved further away from the dominance of Judeo/Christian religious influences and closer to a more secularized view of humanity's individual sovereignty.

The natural rights Americans enjoyed were ideologically separated from the idea of those rights being endowed by a Creator. Instead, the natural rights of humanity were declared to be entitlements consistent with humanity's biological and intellectual supremacy. Part of that supremacy entitled individuals to the right of control over their own person – including the right to consume anything that they, as individuals, desired.

Personal liberty was separated from any form of societal responsibility except perhaps when a person's individual behavior impaired someone else's individual liberty. Economic growth immediately after World War II fostered a new era of consumption as Americans began fulfilling pent up desires left over from the Great Depression and Wartime economies.

More people had their own car. More families had their own home and the technology of convenient time-saving appliances promised more leisure time to enjoy the things Americans purchased. Sexual freedom accompanied the rapid development of individual liberties and it was disassociated from the moral restrictions of religion. Instead, sexual gratification was only limited to the care necessary to avoid disease (though this too was underestimated) or the indignation of outdated "religious" morals.

By the 1960's abortions in America still carried a social stigma but that was rapidly diminishing. Instead there was a great concern to make the procedure safe and legal. The idea of its legality was predicated on the rather new idea that individual liberty extended to a woman's right to treat the child within her as an integrated part of her own body. To do so, the child had to be dehumanized and clinically objectified.

Congress was unable to gain consensus on the issue. The Supreme Court, however, finally had the opportunity to establish an argument supporting this new right by taking the Roe v. Wade case. Rather than simply establishing whether a woman had a straight-forward right to control the life of the unborn child growing in her womb, the Court produced a decision that, without legal or medical precedent, divided the life of the unborn child into three trimesters. The Court ruled that women had the right to abort what was now defined as the fetus up to the end of the second trimester.

In other words, the Supreme Court dehumanized and objectified the unborn for six months but magically considered "it" to be human for the last three months of a pregnancy. Since then there have been other laws passed by Congress that allow abortions to take place even in the last trimester if it is determined that the abortion will save the life of the mother.

American Christians have strong theological grounds for their opposition to abortion at any stage and, frankly, for any reason as well. That has been covered by many books and authors already. Here, however, is a look at the economic impact of those lost human lives who would have otherwise become citizens. This is certainly not to diminish the moral question but to illustrate how terribly this decision has impacted America's ability to organically grow its economy and sustain those Americans among us who have reached the age of retirement.

American abortions from 1970 through 2005 (36 years) totaled 38,507,550. From a purely statistical analysis one cannot help but wonder how many of the 38.5 million humans now dead could have become a Bill Gates, an Abraham Lincoln or a Mother Theresa. Would one of these humans excel beyond the record breaking athletic achievements of a Michael Jordan? What about the millions of dollars these humans would have contributed to our economy? What would the nation's GDP (gross domestic product) look like today if we were a nation of 338 million people instead of just 300 million? How many more cars would be sold? Houses? How many other children would be born to the dead humans if they had been allowed the chance to live and exercise their own natural rights?

Let's look at some simplified numbers. Imagine that we consider only those humans aborted between 1970 and 1999 (30 years) because someone born in 1999 would be 21 or 22 years old in 2010 and therefore able to work, marry and have children. Those born in 1970 would be 39 or 40 now and might already have children of their own. During the years 1970 to 1999 approximately 21.4 million humans were aborted. Let's assume that they were evenly divided between males and females and that as of today about 73% are married (About 27% of Americans filed single tax returns in 2008). That would equal about 7.8 million couples.

If these couples now earned the 2008 median annual income of $44,389, that would translate to $346 billion per year in income to the federal tax rolls. With a nominal tax rate of 10% that would generate almost $35 billion per year in additional tax revenue. As you likely know this analysis is very simplistic. It doesn't even account for the velocity of money in the economy. Velocity is the number of times a dollar is re-spent in the economy. If the 7.8 million couples added a proportionate amount of growth to the nation's gross domestic product, the nation's GDP would be about $15 trillion per year today rather than the estimated $14.5 trillion.

Those American citizens that are now reaching the age of retirement are in fear that the Social Security System will fail during their retirement. One of the reasons America is behind on its obligations to the elderly is that there are 38.5 billion fewer humans contributing to the economy because they were aborted.

Pro-choice advocates will correctly point out that the legalization of abortion only marginally increased the number of abortions. Most, they say, would have occurred anyway – but in conditions like those of a back alley and by practitioners without proper credentials. From a Christian point of view the number of abortions, whether done illegally or legally, is still a violation of an individual's natural rights.

The fact that a woman (as opposed to a man) bears an infant within her body is not theological justification enough to grant a woman rights that are not hers but the Sovereign right of the Creator. Individual sovereignty, an endowment from God, isn't diminished for a man simply because he has no uterus. Our natural rights are equal regardless of gender. Furthermore, the rights of the fetus/baby in the womb are theologically equal to those of the parents.

This theology is predicated on one simple but overpowering argument from the Bible: God became man and was born of a virgin. In the biblical account, the angel Gabriel visits Mary with the announcement that she will conceive and that the child will be the Savior/Messiah. During the early stages of her pregnancy Gabriel visits Mary's betrothed husband, Joseph, as well. Gabriel tells Joseph that the child within Mary's womb is from God.

Having this clear statement about the value and viability of a soul that is within the womb, Christians cannot support a woman's right to choose abortion to the exclusion of the rights of the human father or the even **superior rights of our heavenly Father**. This is why American Christians must support the elimination of a woman's right to an abortion except in those very rare cases where the life of the mother is truly at stake.

While rape and incest are often used as additional cases where abortion is considered justified there is no biblical support for this view since the life within the womb has come into existence through the Sovereign will of God. Likewise unborn children, who have been determined through genetic testing to be at risk of deformations or disabilities, remain under the protection of God's Sovereignty as well.

While it is true that abortion violates the rights of the child, the father and God, it is the violation of God's Sovereign right that has "theological jurisdiction" and this jurisdiction supersedes the jurisdiction of any human court of law. This jurisdiction must be left to God because the aborting of a life within the womb has the same essential moral equivalence as suicide.

While within the womb, the life of an unborn child is completely dependent on the life of the mother. Once it is born, society can provide care for the child. But before it is born, a fetus does not possess constructive self-determination. Therefore, the termination of the life must be through the constructive operation of the woman's will. Whenever a woman aborts a child, it a choice that openly defies the will of God. It is very much like the decision to commit suicide in that it is the ultimate decision of defiance against God (if it is carried out with a sound mind) where the intent is clearly to superimpose one's will against that of God's.

There is no point in prosecuting a suicide and there is equally no point in prosecuting a woman who aborts a child. Judgment, in this case, is sure but it should come from God himself rather than from society's judicial system. Abortions fall into a unique category of crime because the perpetrator of the crime is also the victim in terms that only God can judge.

Society, for the sake of national accountability to God, should have laws against abortion. Society should also vigorously enforce those laws as evidence to God that we accept our societal obligation to respect his Sovereignty. Enforcement would mean prosecuting those who perform abortions without a legitimate (legal) reason.

Congress has struggled with the knowledge that Americans feel very strongly about the issue of pro-choice vs. pro-life. Polling data reveals that the framing of the question itself swings the outcome one way or the other. When taken together the polls indicate that when asked whether or not abortion should be illegal in MOST cases, the majority of Americans say yes. However, the margin is generally within the polls' margins for error and there are polls that indicate that most Americans favor legalized abortion in most cases. In any case, the sides are so nearly even that nothing is being done one way or the other.

A clear minority of Americans think abortion should be legal in ALL cases. However, a similar minority think it should be illegal in ALL cases. As far as Christians are concerned, the issue isn't one where polling data matters much. It is a theological issue where principle outweighs opinion.

The difficult argument is how laws against abortion should be enforced. Should women be charged with murder when they abort their child? The purest ideologue might argue they should be charged with murder but the more accurate theological position for the Christian is to rely on the infinitely more judicious wisdom of God.

Final Thoughts

This brings an end to an attempt to use Christian theology to develop cogent economic and political policy. It cannot be exhaustive but the hope is that it is complete enough to form a guide from which other issues can be tackled by the reader.

Research supporting some issues has not been footnoted to save space and publishing expenses but I have cited data where it has been used. Some Christians may not feel as though I have used enough Scripture to support every argument. There is a reason for that. The fact is that Scripture can be used to justify anything if it is quoted selectively.

My theological views are developed from the discipline of "Biblical Theology." This discipline is predicated on two important things. The first is that Christian theology must be developed from the entirety of Scripture as a whole unit. This forces one to take into account all of God's revelation but it does leave the interpretation of that revelation open for reasonable debate. Theologies based on segmenting Scripture into ages or eras (like dispensational theology) are too restrictive in framing every biblical event into an artificial construct.

Theologies that are called systematic are useful but they are beholden to an overuse of logic and therefore often fail to reveal elements of theology that are completely based on faith. This brings me to the second thing upon which "Biblical Theology" is based. It is based on a predisposition of belief. In other words, biblical theologians are believers first and analysts second. We do not approach Scripture as an independent cynic. We do not use logical contrivances like whether or not a particular passage is culturally relevant or historically consistent with the style of writings from common eras.

Some would have Christians believe that the Bible is just another book and that it should be subjected to critical analysis (including analysis that considers whether a recorded event is logically possible – like miracles). The strength of biblical theology is that its theologians come to the Bible with a deep belief that it is God's own words divinely filtered over the tapestry of human lives. These human lives are real people who wrote as they received inspiration and as they made the best logical sense of what they witnessed. At the end, however, the writers of the Bible were men of faith.

This completes the second book in a trilogy that is still under construction. The first book,

Journey to Unity: The Path to a New American Majority, discussed in detail the basis from which Christians develop an economic and political policy consistent with Christian theology. It is a call to greater biblical literacy among Christians and a call to unify together around those policies that are consistently "Christian."

I hope you have found this book to faithfully address specific issues with reasonable specificity. Thanks for taking the time to read it. Please look for the third book, which should be available by the end of 2010. In this work, I will explore the world of faith more deeply by showing how it is faith that opens the human heart and mind to those dimensions where God exists outside of our four dimensions of time and space. There will be a great deal of both Scripture and theoretical physics discussed.

Finally, my fourth work is also underway and is, for the first time, a fictional novel entitled, *Tapestry*. This book will explore the results of my third work on faith with a storyline that takes you back to the 16th Century to uncover the mystery of a missing tapestry by the artist Rafael. The tapestry reveals a discovery about faith that you won't want to miss.

www.ingramcontent.com/pod-product-compliance
Lightning Source LLC
Chambersburg PA
CBHW062142280526
45788CB00001B/271

* 9 7 8 1 4 5 3 7 6 0 2 6 0 *